Inclusion and the Power of the Individual

in the Teachings of
The Lubavitcher Rebbe

Rabbi Ari Sollish

Inclusion and the Power of the Individual

in the Teachings of

The Lubavitcher Rebbe

INCLUSION
AND THE POWER OF
THE INDIVIDUAL

Published & Copyright © 2019 by
EZRA PRESS
770 Eastern Parkway, Brooklyn, New York 11213
718-774-4000 / Fax 718-774-2718
editor@kehot.com

In cooperation with the
Ruderman Chabad Inclusion Intiative
a project of **Machne Israel**

Order Department:
291 Kingston Avenue, Brooklyn, New York 11213
718-778-0226 / Fax 718-778-4148
www.kehot.com

EZRA PRESS is an imprint of Kehot Publication Society.
The Ezra logo is a trademark of Kehot Publication Society.

1 3 5 7 9 10 8 6 4 2

ISBN: 978-0-8266-9007-4

Printed in The United States of America

Dedicated to

The Rebbe's "Generals"

❦

Jay Ruderman,
Ruderman Family Foundation

The Ruderman Family Foundation, has, with
compassion and vision, changed the landscape of
the global Jewish community. Drawing on their
own inspiration and echoing the wisdom of the
Rebbe who decades ago advocated on behalf of
adults and children with disabilities ("my generals"),
the Ruderman Family Foundation has become a
true champion of inclusion and the power of the
individual.

The Rebbe

The Lubavitcher Rebbe, Rabbi Menachem Mendel Schneerson (1902–1994), of righteous memory, was the seventh leader in the Chabad-Lubavitch dynasty.

He is considered one of the most influential religious personalities of modern times.

People of all faiths, nationalities and backgrounds sought his advice and counsel, traveling from across the world to receive his blessing and guidance.

More than any other individual, the Rebbe was responsible for stirring the conscience of world Jewry, leading to a spiritual awakening that continues to be felt today.

To his hundreds of thousands of followers and millions of admirers around the world, he was—and remains today, following his passing—"the Rebbe."

Contents

Preface

We are gratified to present *Inclusion and the Power of the Individual in the Teachings of the Lubavitcher Rebbe, Rabbi Menachem M. Schneerson.*

Culled from his talks, correspondence and interactions, this work highlights the Rebbe's perspective on the value and importance of embracing, empowering and advocating for those with disabilities.

The work was compiled and written by Rabbi Ari Sollish. A special thank you is due to Jewish Educational Media and the Rohr Jewish Learning Institute for providing valuable resources that were instrumental in the creation of this book, including JEM's My Encounter project and JLI's Toward Inclusion course.

Thank you to Rabbis Yirmi Berkowitz, Yosef B. Friedman, Dovid Olidort, Avraham D. Vaisfiche and Mendel Laine for overseeing and contributing to this work.

Ezra Press

Erev Shabbat, 3 Tammuz 5779
25th Yahrtzeit of the Rebbe
Brooklyn, New York

Foreword

By Mr. Jay Ruderman

President of the Ruderman Family Foundation
Dedicated to Promoting Inclusion
of People with Disabilities

My father, Morton Ruderman, of blessed memory, founded the Ruderman Family Foundation in the early 2000s. He had long been giving back to the local Jewish community in Boston. But when he decided to make a major gift to local Jewish day schools and we started working with the school system, our family realized that there was a fundamental problem in our community that simply wasn't being addressed.

Children with disabilities were being denied access to the most basic and essential Jewish opportunities.

The absence of children with disabilities in Jewish day schools was an affront to our Jewish values. This was a fundamental issue of fairness. We strongly believed that every child should be included and given the same educational opportunities.

We soon realized that this systemic exclusion did not just apply to children and was not just limited to our local area. In Jewish communities around the world, people with disabilities—both children and adults—were not being included in communal life.

We resolved to take up this important cause.

In 2008, I was appointed to head up the Ruderman Family Foundation and began extending the efforts of our foundation to champion the cause of inclusion. Since that time, a major focus of our efforts has been on correcting the injustice of exclusion. We are committed to the inclusion of children and adults with disabilities as a Jewish obligation.

Inclusion, we believe, is an imperative of a flourishing Jewish community. We believe that all people with disabilities can be included in all aspects of community life. We don't limit the definition of disability, and we take an approach that considers the full human lifespan.

We believe a child with Down syndrome belongs in a Jewish day school. A person who is blind or deaf should be able to attend a synagogue service. A person in a wheelchair should have access to a mikveh. Any person with any disability belongs in every aspect of our society.

As I learned more about the Chabad-Lubavitch movement and the teachings of the Lubavitcher Rebbe, Rabbi Menachem Mendel Schneerson, of righteous memory, I realized that this approach of inclusiveness is aligned with the Rebbe's message that *every single person is important and that no one should be excluded.*

I remember walking through a Chabad House and seeing a video playing on a screen. It was from December 1989, filmed at Chabad-Lubavitch world headquarters at 770 Eastern Parkway in Brooklyn, and the Rebbe was handing out a dollar bill to everyone and offering a blessing. He met with a father, mother, and son. The father explained that he had another son in England who had autism, and the Rebbe replied that people with disabilities are very spiritual and have a close connection to G-d.

The Rebbe valued the role that each person has and saw each individual as an integral part of who we are as a people and a society. Each person is made in G-d's image. Each person has a purpose. Each person has the ability to connect spiritually.

The Rebbe taught this, shared this, and encouraged others to follow his lead. The Rebbe was a visionary. He was ahead of his time in understanding the meaning and value of inclusion. This book presents the Rebbe's call for inclusion—a call that each of us can take to heart.

The simple goal of inclusion is to ensure that each person is included in all aspects of life: Attending synagogues, living in the community, participating in the workforce and at school—and everywhere else.

We can and must create and nurture inclusive communities and an inclusive society. When we do so, we will be following the beautiful path that the Rebbe set before us.

Jay Ruderman
President
Ruderman Family Foundation

Introduction

Rabbi Menachem Mendel Schneerson, the Lubavitcher Rebbe, of righteous memory, was a pioneer in inclusion.

At a time when exclusion was the norm, when people with disabilities were essentially locked out of "mainstream" schools, the workforce, and society at large, when families with loved ones who were not deemed "typical" often splintered due to social pressures and stigma, the Rebbe advocated and called for inclusion. With love, compassion, and respect, the Rebbe drew in those whom society all too often pushed away.

Perhaps the most remarkable aspect of the Rebbe's approach to inclusion was how perfectly natural it was to him. The Rebbe's call for inclusion did not result from the latest medical studies, societal shifts, or external pressures; it came from within. Inclusive, to the Rebbe, was the perfectly natural way to be. The only way to be.

This book tells the story of the Rebbe's perspective

on, and advocacy for, inclusion by recounting his teachings, writings, and conversations on this topic throughout the four decades of his public leadership of the Chabad-Lubavitch movement. The Rebbe's message was clear, steadfast, and unwavering:

Every single human being is worthy of dignity, respect, love, and inclusion.

❧

To fully appreciate the unique nature of the Rebbe's call for inclusion, it is helpful to understand how societies historically dealt with disability.

From the earliest of times, people who were not deemed "typical" were demonized and dehumanized. They were cast out, shamed, abused, harmed, and even murdered. Ancient Greek and Roman civilizations canonized into law the killing—or, as they called it, "letting die"—of babies born with deformities. More enlightened societies that were loath to commit acts of violence toward people with disabilities nonetheless had no compunction about demeaning and shaming them.

Throughout history's long and dramatic arc, societies slowly progressed, and became more civilized.

More tolerant attitudes pervaded society in the 18th and 19th centuries, and people with disabilities were extended more compassion and dignity than before. Attempts were made to design care plans to help those in need. Yet, the prevailing method of treatment of people with intellectual and developmental disabilities was to send them away to asylums or state-run institutions, where the care often ended up consisting of subduing, constraining, and medicating. For the most part, societal segregation and exclusion were still the norm for people with disabilities, even in "advanced" countries.

In the 1950s, parents and professionals across the United States initiated grassroots efforts to turn the accepted social construct on its head and to advocate for a more inclusionary approach to people with disabilities. The movements calling for normalization and deinstitutionalization gained momentum in the 1960s and '70s. In the decades since, the push for inclusion has gained traction, and these movements have achieved some remarkable successes. New, inclusive laws in the fields of education, business, and civil engineering have been passed, language has been reformed, medical practices have been revamped, and many new accommodations have been made for people with disabilities.

But there's still a long way to go.

✿

One theme that you might hear from people in the field of disability inclusion—whether from people with disabilities themselves or from family, friends, advocates, or professionals—is that the notion of "accommodation" is a good start, but it isn't nearly enough.

Accommodation implies that there is an inherent imbalance in worthiness and value among the parties. It suggests that it is a given that those without disabilities should have access, education, and opportunity, but not those who do have disabilities. The latter do not inherently possess those rights, it implies. Rather, they are being *accommodated*.

Accommodation, on the surface, suggests equality. Listen closely, however, and the very notion whispers inequality.

What emerges from this perspective is that not much has changed in society's underlying perspective of people with disabilities. And though it has evolved over time, humanity's approach to people with disabilities across history shares a common notion. Whether the approach is one of violence, shaming, institutionalizing, medicating, or even accommodating, the underlying perspective is that there is an "us" and there is a "them," and that we are not equal.

Or, to paraphrase one author, "All are equal, but some are more equal than others."

The goal, then, is not *accommodation* but *inclusion*. Inclusion is creating social and societal structures that embrace all, equally—not despite our differences, but precisely because of them.

Fundamentally, inclusion is about seeing equality within diversity. It's about recognizing that although we may not think or act the same, we all share a common core that unites us.

No two people are alike. We are all different. Inclusion demands that we come together despite—and because of—our differences.

Inclusion calls for the reshaping of our social structures to eradicate the borders between ability and disability, and to grant equal access and equal opportunity.

Inclusion means that we reject the notion that society ought to be designed for some and then refashioned to "accommodate" others. Inclusion means that society is set up—from the start—for all, taking into consideration the diversity of individuals that exists within our communities.

The Rebbe championed this nuanced and radical approach to inclusion. The many stories of the Rebbe, and his incredible body of Torah exposition, attest to this fact. The Rebbe taught that although we are all different, we are—inherently, essentially, naturally, and irrevocably—one.

And since we are one, we must treat each other as one.

The Rebbe's model of inclusion calls on us to recognize differences and then embrace the other as an equal. This is predicated on the understanding that we are one, together with and despite our distinctions, and we must therefore treat each other in a way that reflects that unity.

On what basis are we indeed one?

This notion, championed by the Rebbe, has a strong foundation in both classic and mystical Jewish teachings.

On a very pragmatic level, Judaism teaches that we are all one, big, extended family. Therefore, we ought to love and care for each other like family.

It is perfectly natural to care for family. It's not a burden, nor is it radical or extraordinary, or an accommodation. Caring for family is a given—it comes with the territory.

Inclusion means that we look at the other as family, and we take care of family.

The 12th century German mystic and ethicist Rabbi Yehudah Hachassid poignantly expresses this in his work *Sefer Chassidim* (589):

"There are people who are missing an arm, a leg, or eyes, whether from birth or resulting from an affliction. Those physically 'whole' are created to do what is needed for those who are missing limbs. The infant is born unable to walk, and its mother takes care of its needs. So, too, G-d appoints caregivers for the needs of all who are missing limbs.

"Therefore, all Israel are fathers and mothers to each other, as it says [in Deuteronomy 29:9-10, when listing various segments of Israelites], *The heads of your tribes, your elders, your officers—every person of Israel—your children.* It does not say, 'and your children'; rather, it says simply 'your children,' without the conjunction. This means that we should consider every person of Israel to be like our children whom we supply with the necessities they need."

There is yet another biblical allusion to the idea that we all comprise one collective family.

In the fifth chapter of the book of Genesis, the Torah lists the chronicles of the first ten generations of humankind—Adam, Seth, Enosh, Kenan, Mahalalel, Jared, Enoch, Methuselah, Lamech, and Noah. The Torah introduces the list by saying, *This is the narrative of the offspring of Adam.*

Surprisingly, the great work of halachic Midrash, *Sifra*, records the opinion of Ben Azzai, who says that the verse *This is the narrative of the offspring of Adam* is a great fundamental principle of the Torah—greater even than the verse *You shall love your neighbor as yourself.*

What is so impactful about this verse?

The 16th century Biblical commentator and Talmudist Aharon ibn Chaim, in his *Korban Aharon* commentary on *Sifra*, offers a brilliant explanation, linking the verse introducing Adam's offspring to the inherent human responsibility we have toward each other:

"*This is the narrative of the offspring of Adam*—Ben Azzai maintains that this is more fundamental a principle than love of one's fellow. For in saying that all are offspring of one father, and that all are brothers, it follows that no one should act as if he were greater than another, and no one should hate another. The intent of this text is to say that this record—the Torah—is of the offspring of the first man, that all are children of one father. This is what should truly be called a great fundamental principle, for the verse *Love your fellow* requires love only on account of fellowship and friendliness, whereas the verse *This is the narrative* requires love on account of brotherhood, which is a greater obligation."

Our love and care for each other derives not only from our *familiar* bonds—it derives from our *familial* bonds.

This is much more than an obligation. Recognizing our essential familial ties—how we are brothers and sisters to each other, how others are our children—moves our responsibility toward each other into the realm of natural and intuitive.

Inclusion, then, is not some lofty, out of touch, ideal. It is implicit in the way Judaism instructs us to look at each other.

We are one. So we naturally treat each other as one.

There is also a profound mystical approach to the notion of our collective oneness.

The perception that we are distinct from others stems from a body-centric *Weltanschauung*. The differences we perceive are typically physical in nature. Our eyes tell us that this person looks or acts different from us, and our minds conclude that we are therefore different.

Our souls tell another story. Our souls are—as the 18th century founder of the Chabad movement, Rabbi Schneur Zalman of Liadi, writes in his seminal work *Tanya*—"Literally, a piece of G-d." A unified, undivided, piece of G-d. This means that there's no "me" or "you" when it comes to souls. Souls share the same unified Source, the same essential Divine DNA.

Our bodies divide us. Our souls unite us.

In the words of Rabbi Schneur Zalman of Liadi (*Tanya*, Chapter 32):

"There can be no true love and fraternity between those who regard their bodies as primary and their souls secondary... Only one whose sole joy is the joy of the soul can directly and easily fulfill the mitzvah, *You shall love your fellow as yourself.*"

When we approach the world soul-first, when we look at others through the lens of our core spiritual identity, we don't see distinction, and we don't see difference. We see oneness.

And the necessary result of seeing oneness is *inclusion*.

Viewing life from a body-first perspective informs us that there are real and measurable differences between us. At worst, this perspective leads to an attitude of exclusion. *You are different; you don't fit in.* At best, this perspective leads to an attitude of accommodation. *Even though you are different, we'll find a way to let you participate.*

But viewing life from a soul-first perspective informs us that we are innately and essentially one. At the core of our being. From the inside-out.

Recognizing the truth of our core oneness and the sameness of our spirit drives us to naturally include all. For when we feel as one, we act as one.

To the Rebbe, the oneness between human beings was obvious and ever-apparent. He lived by and modeled this soul-truth—that we are all one, inside. That there's so much more that unites us *essentially* than divides us *superficially*.

This perspective is not easy to live by. It's far more intuitive to look at others, judge them by their most external qualities, and put up walls of division and separation.

The soul-first perspective of seeing others as soul-beings is profoundly more difficult. It challenges the very nature of our eyes. The truth of our shared oneness is hidden under many layers of material trappings.

But it's still possible to peel back the layers and see the truth. It's possible to look at someone else and see who they are on the inside, as opposed to what they look like on the outside.

Really, it begins with how we see ourselves. Do we see ourselves as body-first beings or soul-first beings? When we think about ourselves, do we begin with our external qualities or with our deeper, internal qualities? Do we measure ourselves by *what we do* or by *who we are*?

When we appreciate ourselves for who we are on the inside, when we look in the mirror and see our own soul, we can then behold the same soul-essence truth in others.

Throughout his four decades of leadership, the Rebbe spoke incessantly about the theme of Jewish unity and oneness—about seeing ourselves as one. It was a consistent rallying cry, a perspective-shifter, and a call to action. The Rebbe emphasized time and again that we are one united people—not divided individuals.

One such talk took place on March 31, 1990, at a farbrengen, a public gathering, at the Rebbe's synagogue at 770 Eastern Parkway in Brooklyn. The first five chapters of the Book of Leviticus were read from the Torah that day, and for the Haftarah, selections from the forty-third and forty-fourth chapters of Isaiah were read.

The Rebbe illuminated the opening verse of the Haftarah (Isaiah 43:21), *I have created this people for Myself; they shall relate My praise*:

"This is a statement that expresses the unique nature of the Jewish people. Each Jew, man, woman, and child, at every time and in every circumstance, is a member of G-d's nation, created by G-d for a distinct purpose, to 'relate My praise'... Jews, as a nation, despite the differences between them, are a single, indivisible entity united by their essential commitment to G-dliness...

"The Jewish people are a single unified entity. Our

Sages explain that the word Yisrael, ישראל ('Israel') in Hebrew, is an acronym for the Hebrew words יש ששים ריבוא אותיות לתורה, meaning, 'There are 600,000 (the number of Jewish souls) letters in the Torah.' A blemish in a single letter of a Torah scroll disqualifies the entire scroll, including even the Ten Commandments. Similarly, the status of every single member of our people has an effect on the people as a whole...

"From the above, we can appreciate the importance of speaking positively about every Jew and the detrimental effects of speaking critically. The Jewish people are G-d's nation. Therefore, anyone who has true fear of G-d will also fear to criticize the nation who are His children and subjects. Criticizing or speaking unfavorably about any portion of the Jewish people is like making such statements against G-d Himself. Zechariah the prophet relates that a person who strikes a Jew is like one who strikes G-d in the eye..."

In this talk and in numerous others, the Rebbe spoke to our core commonality. We stem from the same source, we contain the same soul-essence, and we share a common purpose.

It is this sense of oneness and unity that drives inclusion—truly, organically, and innately.

The Rebbe was a pioneer in inclusion.

His public talks, letters, and private conversations paint a clear picture of his perspective on inclusion. When exploring this fascinating record, certain inviolable tenets become distilled—tenets that govern our attitude toward, and interaction with, other human beings.

Every person is valuable and must be valued.

Every person is loved by G-d and must be loved.

Every person carries the dignified "image of G-d" and must be granted dignity.

Every person is a unique individual and must be treated individually.

Every person is part of a unified whole and, therefore, we are all one.

What follows are the accounts of the Rebbe's pioneering perspective on inclusion and the power of the individual.

Chapter One

Essence

"Our bodies divide us. Our souls unite us."

—*Tanya, Chapter 32*

Augustus 19, 1976. On an unseasonably cool summer day in New York City, large buses quietly pull up to the iconic basement synagogue in the Crown Heights neighborhood of Brooklyn. Known simply as "770," this is the synagogue of Rabbi Menachem Mendel Schneerson, the Lubavitcher Rebbe, spiritual leader of the Chabad-Lubavitch movement.

Coming to meet the Rebbe this day are a diverse group of Israeli war veterans. These veterans span the full range of religious affiliation and identification. Some are familiar with the Rebbe and his teachings. Many are not. Truthfully, more than a few are hesitant to spend several hours visiting a Chasidic rabbi in Brooklyn. They are here only due to the persuasion of others in the group.

Despite their religious and theological differences, there is something that unites them. What is common to all of them is their physical condition.

Each has an injury or disability.

They are in the United States on the tail end of a multi-week trip organized by the Israel Defense Force Disabled Veterans Organization. The trip began with a stay in Toronto, where they represented their country at the fifth Paralympic Games. Now, with the games concluded—and with the Israeli team coming in third in the overall medal count—the Israeli delegation has made its way to New York.

The veterans begin filing into the synagogue.

770 is a cavernous space. The synagogue, usually filled with hundreds or even thousands of people praying and studying, is on this day almost entirely empty and quiet. It has been prepared and designated for the honored guests.

The visiting Israeli veterans take their place at wooden benches set facing a long stage.

The Rebbe walks in. His sense of purpose is unmistakable. He sits down at the center of the table. His presence commands respect and attention. Like a general. Like royalty.

Immediately, the Rebbe puts his guests at ease, warmly

greeting and acknowledging each of them. He makes eye contact with them. His smile radiates an authentic love and camaraderie.

For a group of people who are used to receiving stares and looks of pity and even revulsion, the Rebbe's loving welcome is uplifting, transformative, and healing.

ℎ

Mr. Joseph Cabiliv was one of those whose lives were transformed that day—which is all the more incredible considering that he hadn't even wanted to go to 770 to meet the Rebbe in the first place.

Joseph was an Israeli war veteran who had sustained serious injuries in his service. His legs had been severely crushed when his military jeep was rocked by an old Syrian land mine in the Golan Heights. Two of his fellow soldiers were killed instantly in the blast. Doctors had tried to save his legs. They couldn't.

Compounding his physical injuries was the emotional pain. Joseph felt alone. No one, it seemed, knew what to say or do to ease his pain.

Recovering in Haifa's Rambam Hospital, his mother

would come over to his bed and cry uncontrollably, so much so that he would have to console her. His father, at the other extreme, would sit at his bedside in perfect silence.

Which was worse, he wondered—his mother's tears or his father's silence?

Friends would visit him, but they too didn't really know what to say. Sure, they engaged him in small talk. But beneath their cheery façade, he knew they were profoundly uncomfortable. He knew this because when they would speak with him they would never look him in the eye.

His return to civilian life was fraught with difficulty. He could not resume his job as a welder, and no one seemed to have a job for a man without legs. When out in public he felt like an outcast. People kept their distance when he ventured out in his wheelchair. Large, empty spaces magically opened up around him on even the busiest street corners.

When Joseph heard about the opportunity to meet with the Rebbe, he was skeptical. What could the Rebbe possibly say or do to help him? But in those first few moments with the Rebbe, seeing how the Rebbe looked at him with love and gratitude and genuine respect, Joseph's inner pain melted away.

For the first time since returning from war, he felt understood, valued, and loved unconditionally.

With one look of the Rebbe, Joseph's life changed.

"From that terrible day on which I had woken without my legs in the Rambam Hospital, I had seen all sorts of things in the eyes of those who looked at me: pain, pity, revulsion, anger. But this was the first time in all those years that I encountered true empathy. With that glance that scarcely lasted a second and the faint smile on his lips, the Rebbe conveyed to me that he is with me—utterly and exclusively."

Joseph no longer felt alone.

The Rebbe begins his formal address to his Israeli guests. Out of respect for their native tongue, the Rebbe speaks to them in Hebrew, and not in his customary Yiddish.

He opens his talk on the topic of camaraderie and friendship, and on the notion of essential Jewish unity.

"When Jews from different places and different countries meet, it is not a case of distinct individuals who are meeting by chance. Quite the contrary: it is one unified

body, one people, who happen to be dispersed. And when they meet, the truth is revealed—that they are indeed one people, despite their being scattered in the diaspora, or in different parts of the Holy Land."

Jews are unified in a manner that transcends time and space, the Rebbe explains. Whether from Israel or the United States, Jews are essentially one, due to the spiritual connection between them that remains uncompromised by material and earthly limitations.

The physical may divide us. But the spiritual unites us.

The Rebbe explains that the spiritual reality at the essence of the Jew has enabled the Jewish people to triumph and persevere throughout time, and across history. Even when their bodies were tormented, broken, and beaten.

Spirit triumphs over matter. Soul triumphs over body.

This is not simply a historical truth, continues the Rebbe. This is a personal truth as well.

A human being is much more than a body. A human being, fundamentally, is a soul—a soul that for a limited amount of time makes use of a limited space called a body. To define a person by the body is to miss out entirely on what a person is truly about.

Human beings are souls with bodies—not bodies with souls.

The Rebbe's message reverberates throughout the room. He is speaking to a group of Israeli veterans who have physical injuries, speaking directly to their hearts, delivering a strong and clear message of who they truly are and how they ought to view themselves.

You are a soul in a body—not a body with a soul. Yes, you can choose to focus on the apparent deficiencies of your body, but that would be making the secondary primary. The truest way to see yourself is to look at the gifts of your soul.

"When, for some reason, a person is lacking in something quantitatively," says the Rebbe, "it is no reason at all to be dejected, G-d forbid. Quite the contrary: Since he is lacking something physically—by no fault of his own, or through doing a good deed, and especially through sacrificing himself in defense of the Jewish people in a particular place, and particularly in the Holy Land—this is proof positive that the Creator has endowed him or her with unique spiritual abilities. These abilities enable him or her to overcome that which ordinary eyes perceive as a physical, bodily deficiency, and shows that, in fact, this person is not just equal to all those around him, but moreover, he possesses an additional spirit that allows him to overcome the apparent physical shortcoming."

"It is for this reason that I disapprove of the term 'handicapped' being used for anyone, as this suggests some type of inferiority. On the contrary, we must emphasize *that he is unique and exceptional, possessing unique abilities granted by the Creator, above and beyond the capacity of others. This enables him to overcome hardships and obstacles that others cannot overcome.*

"Therefore, in keeping with the 'Jewish custom' to offer advice even in areas that are not one's business, I would like to suggest that the name be changed from 'the disabled of Israel' to the 'exceptional of Israel'—whether exceptional by cause of war, or otherwise. This is not merely semantics; rather, it describes the situation in the truest way."

M r. Yosef Lautenberg was the leader of this Israeli delegation to the Toronto Paralympic Games in 1976.

Yosef had been injured in the battle for Jerusalem during Israel's War of Independence in 1948. From that point on, he made it his life's mission to advocate and care for the needs of wounded Israeli veterans.

He was one of the founders of the Israeli Defense Force Disabled Veterans Organization, an organization created in the wake of the War of Independence to provide wounded Israeli veterans with all their needs for their long rehabilitation process. He was also the founder of Beit Halochem, a sports, rehabilitation, and recreation center serving wounded Israeli veterans and their families.

Yosef Lautenberg was also instrumental in the 1976 Israeli delegation's visit with the Rebbe. It was he who had come up with the idea to take the group to meet with the Rebbe, and it was he who had made the phone calls to the Rebbe's secretariat to arrange the details of the visit.

In reflecting on that time, Yosef recalls the tremendous emotion that was felt at that gathering. He, along with the others, felt the Rebbe's love, respect, and empathy.

"Some of us were traditional Jews, some non-traditional, but everybody embraced this meeting with the Rebbe. We were all very moved by it. We sat there transfixed, listening to his talk."

The Rebbe's message of viewing people based on their soul-ability and not based on their body-disability made a powerful impact on him:

"As a person who has spent my entire life in this field, I can tell you that the Rebbe's words have been a guiding light for me. I've met people injured in the worst way—blinded, paralyzed—and with the little bit they had, they achieved the greatest accomplishments one could imagine.

"Someone who doesn't know this field would never believe it. But the Rebbe understood this immediately when he met with us, and this spoke to us in an exceptional way."

⚜

This encounter magnificently captures the Rebbe's perspective on how we ought to look at another human being—which serves as a foundational tenet of inclusion.

It's easy to size up a person based on their appearance, dress, body, or perceived "ability." It's easy to focus on what a person might be missing, or on what they perhaps cannot do.

But the Rebbe taught—by shining example—that we ought to rather look at the *essence* of a human being. Instead of focusing on and assessing physical ability, we ought to recognize the true, inner gifts that a person possesses.

This represents a monumental shift. The shift from looking at what a person can or cannot *do*, to looking at who a person *is*. The shift from looking at *ability*, to looking at *identity*.

The Rebbe refused to see people through a purely utilitarian lens. Objects have utility. Human beings have inner, majestic, infinite value.

All human beings.

This is what so greatly impacted and uplifted the visiting Israeli veterans. Many, by their own telling, had come into that encounter disillusioned and depressed. They struggled with their injuries. They struggled with the new ways in which they were required to live. They struggled with people's acceptance of them, and with their acceptance of themselves.

Then they experienced the way that the Rebbe spoke to them, the way that the Rebbe saw them. As human beings. With infinite, essential value.

There is nothing more life-affirming than seeing yourself through the eyes of someone who values you essentially and unconditionally.

For Joseph Cabiliv, it was his personal encounter with the Rebbe following the talk that confirmed his newly empowered sense of self.

"In parting, the Rebbe gave each of us a dollar bill, in

order—he explained—that we give it to charity on his behalf, making us partners in the fulfillment of a mitzvah. He walked from wheelchair to wheelchair, shaking our hands, giving each a dollar, and adding a personal word or two. When my turn came, I saw his face up close and I felt like a child. He gazed deeply into my eyes, took my hand between his own, pressed it firmly, and said, 'Thank you,' with a slight nod of his head.

"I later learned that he had said something different to each one of us. To me he said, 'Thank you.' Somehow, he sensed that that was exactly what I needed to hear. With those two words, the Rebbe erased all the bitterness and despair that had accumulated in my heart. I carried the Rebbe's 'thank you' back to Israel, and I carry it with me to this very day."

Joseph went on to enjoy a successful career in real estate. But he never forgot the gift the Rebbe gave him—the gift of feeling loved, respected, and valued. The gift of being seen for who he truly was.

Loving, respecting, and valuing others— *essentially*—is at the heart of inclusion.

Inclusion is not an accommodation, going out of one's way to find place for another in spite of their "condition." That is often felt by the person being accommodated as disrespectful.

Inclusion, rather, means that we love, value, and respect each and every human being essentially and wholly. And because of that, we organically and intuitively include all.

For when we genuinely love, value, and respect another, inclusion comes naturally.

Chapter Two

Positivity

"Think good and it will be good."
—Rabbi Menachem Mendel of Lubavitch, the Tzemach Tzedek

In 2004, Helena Oliver reaches out to Israeli Professor Reuven Feuerstein. Helena is from England. Although she has never met Professor Feuerstein, she believes him to be her only hope.

What she's looking for is nothing short of a miracle. And Professor Feuerstein is known to be a "miracle worker."

Helena's son Alex was born with a rare disorder of the blood vessels in his brain, which causes epileptic seizures. Up until the age of seven, Alex's seizures were controlled by powerful medication. But the medication was debilitating in other ways, including hindering his ability to speak.

When Alex turned seven, Helena convened a team of neurologists to explore alternatives. They decided on a plan to surgically remove the damaged left half of his *brain, with the hope that the right half of his brain would begin to function properly.*

The surgery was a success. Alex was taken off the seizure medication, and he slowly began to speak. But even after years in a school for students with disabilities, Alex was unable to read or write.

Helena wishes dearly for her son to read and write, but experts tell her it's an impossibility. After all, the left brain—the part that was removed from Alex—is typically responsible for language acquisition.

Then Helena hears about Professor Feuerstein and the thousands of children around the world whose lives he has changed. These are children whose ability to learn had been written off by doctors, therapists, and experts, and who have experienced miraculous growth under the steady care and guidance of Professor Feuerstein and his team in Jerusalem.

Helena contacts Professor Feuerstein's International Center for the Enhancement of Learning Potential. Soon, she and Alex are in Israel, at the center. Professor Feuerstein administers a unique battery of tests and determines that Alex can indeed be taught to read and write. Helena is overjoyed at the fiercely positive outlook.

It takes less than a year at the center for Alex to make astounding progress. He learns how to read by phonetically decoding words, and he learns how to write beautifully. Just as Professor Feuerstein had predicted.

Part of what makes Professor Feuerstein so successful is his ceaseless optimism—his uncanny ability to see potential when others see hopelessness. This optimism is what drives him to help those whom others have simply written off.

And much of his optimism stems from the interminable positive outlook of the Lubavitcher Rebbe.

"I was asked by people, 'How do you dare tell people that this child will ever be able to speak? How do you dare say that this child will be able to read, finish school, go to yeshivah? *That's not what we expect!'*

"Much of this belief, much of this power of belief, came from my interactions with the Rebbe."

The late Professor Reuven Feuerstein, who passed away in 2014, was a world-renowned clinical and developmental cognitive psychologist, celebrated for his groundbreaking work in demonstrating that intelligence is not fixed but modifiable. He founded his revolutionary learning methods on the premise that intelligence is a variable that can be developed at every stage of life.

"Human beings," insisted Feuerstein, "have the unique characteristic of being able to modify themselves no matter how they start out. A person can overcome even inborn barriers and traumas."

Throughout his nearly six decades of clinical practice, Professor Feuerstein worked with thousands of people with intellectual disabilities or traumatic brain injuries, helping them learn how to learn, communicate, and live independently. Families came from around the world to seek help for their children and loved ones. These were people whom others had given up hope on, but Professor Feuerstein always found a way to help.

Often, as in the story of Alex Oliver, what he helped people achieve was simply miraculous.

There was the child who was brought to him with an IQ of 60, who eventually became a drama teacher. There was the boy from France who was diagnosed as a non-speaking autistic, who learned to speak in just a few weeks. Then there was Jason Kingsley, a young man with Down syndrome, who went on to co-author the book *Count Us In: Growing Up with Down Syndrome.*

"Our methods are based on the idea that every person has a healthy part," Professor Feuerstein explained. "We are not looking for the pathological part, the weakness, but the strength. We believe in reshaping the person through accessing his healthy part."

Professor Feuerstein credited the Rebbe with helping him maintain his incredible sense of positivity and the unwavering belief that he could help people reach goals that others deemed impossible. The Rebbe regularly referred children to him, and, time and again, reminded him not to give up on anyone.

"I must say," said Professor Feuerstein, "to believe that such a thing is possible—the idea that people with genetic disorders, chromosomal disorders, can be turned into high functioning, normal functioning individuals, and can be brought very close to study, to Judaism—I got it very much from the Rebbe."

In 1992, Professor Feuerstein was awarded the Israel Prize for Social Sciences. In 2012, he was nominated for the Nobel Peace Prize. His success was due, in no small measure, to his hopeful, positive attitude toward others. An attitude he learned from the Rebbe.

"Psychology, as it is today," said Professor Feuerstein, "is very limited in our understanding of the other. It is very much affected by and related to our understanding of ourselves. In the way the Rebbe understood the condition of the individual, and the way he claimed and suggested and felt empowered to say, 'Yes, do it!' there was a different way of seeing the human being. Not as a reflection of yourself, but as something that comes from a G-dly source above."

*M*rs. *Chana Sharfstein has endured more than her fair share of heartbreak.*

Her father is brutally murdered in a random act of violence while walking in a Boston park.

Just five years later, her mother passes too.

At the age of 25, she is an orphan.

But Chana has her own family to raise. She is married, with two small children.

On January 15, 1961, she gives birth to a baby girl, her third child. She names the baby Zlata Esther, after her mother and mother-in-law.

Zlatie, as she is affectionately known, is a happy baby.

Her parents and siblings love her dearly. But as the months go by, Chana grows concerned.

Zlatie is different from the other children. While they are exuberant and energetic, Zlatie is very quiet and undemanding. She rarely cries and doesn't ask to be picked up. She is content to remain in her crib and playpen. She is calm. Almost too calm. And that concerns her mother.

The pediatrician reassures her that everything is fine. But at eighteen months, unable to shake her concerns, Chana takes Zlatie to Presbyterian Hospital in New York City for neurological testing.

The tests come back inconclusive, but a prominent psychiatrist gives a diagnosis.

Autism.

Chana has never heard of autism. Neither has her pediatrician. She does not know what autism is, or what it means for her daughter.

Very little, in fact, is known about autism in 1964. And there's as much misinformation circulating as there is information.

To Chana, the diagnosis comes as a shock. She is concerned. She is frightened. What type of care will Zlatie need? Will she be able to provide that care for her daughter?

Her heart is filled with fear, sadness, anguish, anger, and an acute sense of helplessness.

In this moment of confusion, Chana has someone to turn to: the Rebbe.

Chana's family has a long-standing relationship with the Rebbe.

Her father, Rabbi Yaakov Yisroel Zuber, had studied in the renowned yeshivah *in Lubavitch, and had served as a Chabad rabbi in Stockholm, Sweden, during World War II, before moving to Boston.*

Chana, too, has a personal relationship with the Rebbe.

It was the Rebbe who had comforted her after the loss of her father and mother. It was the Rebbe who had gently advised and guided her when she was looking for a husband, counseling her on the meaning of true love and what to look for in a prospective spouse.

To her, the Rebbe is a father figure. And so, learning of Zlatie's diagnosis, she turns to the Rebbe for fatherly advice, for guidance. Little Zlatie walks beside her, holding her hand, as she steps into the Rebbe's office. They sit down, and Chana pours out her heart.

She tells the Rebbe that her little girl has autism. She voices her concerns. Her fears. When she finishes, she waits for the Rebbe's response.

The Rebbe pulls out a piece of paper and a pencil from his desk drawer. He pushes it across the desk, toward Zlatie, who is sitting in a chair next to her mother.

Zlatie picks up the pencil and begins scribbling on the paper. The Rebbe smiles.

"I don't know why they are making such a big deal about her," he says, continuing to smile. "The way she is reacting is perfectly normal."

The Rebbe's words soothe Chana's heart. They lift her spirit and fill her with hope. The Rebbe's optimism and positivity cut through the confusion she has felt inside, and help her discover her courage and determination.

The Rebbe again reaches into his desk drawer, this time pulling out a silver dollar. He holds it in front of Zlatie. She immediately extends her hand and takes the coin from him. The Rebbe smiles once more.

Before their meeting is done, the Rebbe offers Chana some practical suggestions. One of them is to enroll Zlatie in a nursery school. This, the Rebbe says, will help her advance and develop, as she will be learning from the children around her.

The meeting is transformational for Chana.

"When I returned home," she says, "I realized that the Rebbe had given me courage and hope. He had implied

that there was a lot that I could do with my child. In retrospect, had he not conveyed that message, I would not have bothered to do as much as I did with Zlatie. But because he validated her potential, pointing out that she was reacting normally, he gave me tremendous hope. I needed that hope, and I needed that courage to keep going.

"When she refused to speak, I worked with her until she did. I taught her blessings, which she recited before eating, and I made sure that every opportunity available to her was maximized, even though there was not much in terms of therapy in those days. I was able to do all that because of the Rebbe's encouragement. He saw a striving soul in my daughter and, because he did, so did I."

The Rebbe was a fervent optimist. He forever saw the beauty, goodness, light, and potential in others. He believed in others—*truly believed*—even when no one else did. Even when they didn't believe in themselves.

The Rebbe believed in Zlatie Sharfstein. And he taught her mother how to believe in her as well.

The Rebbe taught Chana to see her daughter's

potential. To pay attention to her progress. To recognize her success. And to work hard to help her realize even more success.

This is a fundamental shift in perspective. It's focusing less on the challenges, and more on the opportunities. It's paying attention not to the setbacks, but to the victories. And being motivated by each and every victory.

At its core, this is an attitude of fierce positivity and hopefulness.

You can focus on what a person might lack. Or you can focus on the gifts they possess and on the potential they hold.

The Rebbe modeled the latter approach, displaying and advocating an attitude of positivity.

Chana Sharfstein saw the value in this attitude. Focusing on the positive and believing in her daughter positively impacted both of their lives.

Naturally, maintaining a positive and optimistic attitude about others leads us toward inclusion. After all, when you believe in someone, you don't exclude them. You include them.

It's not at all surprising, then, that in the very same meeting where the Rebbe encouraged Chana to see the beauty in her daughter, he also encouraged her to enroll her daughter in a nursery school so that she would be around children her age.

The Rebbe looked at every person in the most hopeful and positive light, and he saw within them incredible potential waiting to be nurtured and realized.

And he encouraged and demanded that we all do the same.

The Rebbe's positive and encouraging approach toward people with intellectual and other developmental disabilities profoundly impacted the lives of former Mattel executive Mr. David Mayer and his wife, Lynn.

David and Lynn welcomed their son Avremel into the world in late 1984. Avremel was born with Down syndrome. His parents were initially devastated.

"Anyone who has had this experience," says David, "knows that you first have to go through a mourning process for the child you wanted to have, and then you can start embracing the child G-d gave you. So, both my wife and I were going through a difficult time then."

When Avremel was two-and-a-half months old, David and Lynn flew from their home in Los Angeles to New York City. They stopped in 770, hoping to meet with the Rebbe and receive a blessing for their son.

To their disappointment, a private audience with the Rebbe was not possible at that time. But if they waited outside his office, they learned, they might have the chance to ask for a blessing when the Rebbe returned from the synagogue following the afternoon prayers.

So David, Lynn, and little Avremel waited patiently for the Rebbe's return, hoping to receive a blessing. Indeed, after a short wait, the Rebbe approached.

The encounter was brief. But the impact of what happened in that moment still reverberates today.

David recounts what happened:

"Seeing us standing there, the Rebbe stopped. He looked at our Avremel, took a coin out of his pocket, and put it into the baby's hand. But, because of the Down syndrome, Avremel didn't have the muscle tone to hold onto the coin, and it fell.

"Before I could react, the Rebbe stooped down and picked up the coin from the floor. He put it back into Avremel's hand and this time folded his little fingers around it. Then the Rebbe leaned toward my wife and said, 'These children are my generals. You shouldn't worry.' Then the Rebbe said something more that she couldn't quite make out, but she thought he said, 'He will be a blessing.'"

In that brief encounter, the Rebbe shared with the Mayers a positive perspective about their son. This perspective quite literally changed their lives.

"He is my general. He will be a blessing."

"Avremel is truly special, truly a blessing," David says. "He is the best thing that has ever happened to us. But that is not the way I saw it back then, in February 1985—not until the Rebbe opened my eyes to the gift we had just received from G-d."

Through his unflinchingly positive and inclusive attitude, the Rebbe changed the way people viewed others with disabilities. He also changed the way people with disabilities viewed themselves.

Baruch Wilhelm walked into the Rebbe's office

hoping for a miracle. He got one—but not the one he was expecting.

Baruch grew up in Israel. As a young boy, he suffered an accident that caused damage to his ears, severely limiting his hearing. He went to doctors, but there was nothing that they could do to improve his hearing. He would need to wear hearing aids for the rest of his life.

This was a sharp blow to Baruch. He felt uncomfortable and embarrassed wearing the hearing aids. He worried about what strangers would say. He even worried about what his friends would say. As he grew older, he worried about the future. How would this affect his future marriage prospects? What would a young woman think about a young man who wore hearing aids? Would anyone want to marry him?

These were some of the questions that swirled around in Baruch's mind.

In 1980, Baruch traveled with his family to New York to spend the High Holidays with the Rebbe. In addition to praying in the Rebbe's synagogue and taking part in the Rebbe's public gatherings, the Wilhelm family arranged to have a private meeting with the Rebbe.

Baruch was hopeful. This was his opportunity to request from the Rebbe in person what he wanted more than anything else—a blessing to regain his hearing. He was praying for a miracle. He was counting on a miracle.

Baruch, in fact, had taken out his hearing aids, even though he couldn't hear properly without them. He refused to wear them. He was expecting a blessing from the Rebbe to be able to hear again.

The time for the private meeting arrived. First, Baruch's parents were invited in to the Rebbe's office, alone, without the children. Then, it was Baruch's turn to meet with the Rebbe. He walked into the Rebbe's office holding a letter he penned, asking for a blessing to regain his hearing.

When Baruch recounts his meeting with the Rebbe, tears fill his eyes and he chokes up with emotion. This would be a meeting that would dramatically change his life.

"I entered the Rebbe's office," says Baruch, "and the Rebbe was sitting with his glasses on. I gave him my letter.

"He began reading my letter, and while reading it he said, 'You have to be happy and joyous!' The Rebbe looked up and asked, 'Do you hear me?'

"'Yes,' I replied, 'yes, I hear.'

"The Rebbe said, 'You have to wear the hearing aids, and you will be happy. You'll return to Israel... and you will succeed.'"

"'Rebbe,' I said, 'I would like a blessing to hear well.'

"The Rebbe said, 'Be joyous, and you will succeed!'"

Baruch later learned what the Rebbe had said to his parents before he joined the meeting.

His mother had burst into tears the moment she walked into the Rebbe's office. She told the Rebbe about Baruch's refusal to wear his hearing aids, and how he was relying on the Rebbe's blessing to regain his hearing.

The Rebbe told her:

"He doesn't want to wear the hearing aids because he is embarrassed. I understand. But your Baruch needs to continue wearing them, and they won't lessen his chances of finding a good match. He must be happy and joyous."

Baruch's mother then reiterated that he had taken out his hearing aids in the hope that the Rebbe would bless him to be able to hear. He was holding out for a miracle. "He wants to stay here, in America," she said, "near the Rebbe, until he's able to hear."

The Rebbe gently told her that Baruch should not stay in America. He should return to Israel, where he knows the language and has friends. There, the Rebbe said, he will be happy.

And this is the message the Rebbe told Baruch as well.

Baruch walked out of the Rebbe's room a changed man. He stopped feeling sorry for himself and began to look at himself positively. He began to live life with a sense of happiness and joy. And, as the Rebbe had promised, he succeeded, getting married and raising a beautiful family.

The Rebbe had not given Baruch what he had wanted. The Rebbe had not granted him a blessing for hearing. Instead, the Rebbe had given him perhaps an even greater blessing—a blessing for *seeing*, for seeing himself in a positive light, for seeing the blessings that he had, for seeing the gifts he possessed.

The Rebbe was the catalyst for Baruch to achieve a personal metamorphosis, to feel good about himself, and to live life with inner peace and joy.

This was Baruch's miracle—a miracle that came about through the Rebbe's positive and uplifting attitude.

And it is this radically positive attitude that shapes a healthy and constructive approach to inclusion.

Chapter Three

Love

"The mitzvah to love your fellow as yourself extends to someone you've never met."
—*Rabbi Schneur Zalman of Liadi, the Alter Rebbe*

It is the 1970s and a debate is raging in the field of mental health care. The debate pits neighbor against neighbor, and families against professionals. The subject of the debate concerns how to best care for people with intellectual disabilities.

For as long as anyone can remember, the practice has been to place people with intellectual and other developmental disabilities in the care of state-run institutions. Now, there is a movement to create more inclusionary group homes inside neighborhoods and communities. The belief is that this form of integration and co-living will benefit the individuals in the home.

But there is pushback.

Some are concerned about the benefit and viability of the

group home model for the residents of the home. Some are concerned for the safety of the community. Some are concerned about the impact this will have on local schools.

The Jewish community is not immune to this debate.

On August 9, 1979, Dr. Robert Wilkes, a Jewish social worker working out of Brooklyn's Coney Island Hospi-tal and the chairman of Region II Council for Mental Retardation, *pens a letter to the Rebbe. Dr. Wilkes asks the Rebbe to share the Jewish perspective on the debate regarding how best to care for people with intellectual disabilities.*

"How may we view this issue—that is, caring for indi-viduals who have a disability which requires life-long care and supervision—from a Jewish perspective? As a concerned Jew, I care very much about our Jewish com-munity: how we treat one another and how we conduct ourselves as human beings... I am also aware that there has to be an equal concern for both the individual as well as for one's total community.

"The question is: how do we protect and safeguard all of our Jewish children... so that they can have the opportu-nity to grow, to develop, and to live 'Jewishly'?"

Dr. Wilkes' letter to the Rebbe touches off a series of cor-respondence that continues for a year-and-a-half.

The Rebbe responds to Dr. Wilkes on August 12, 1979, with a lengthy and detailed letter articulating an inclusionary approach to caring for people with disabilities.

The first point the Rebbe presents is the critical importance of maintaining a positive and hopeful attitude.

For the teacher or social worker to realize success, they must see the potential within the person they are working with. They should deem any challenge as only temporary—one that can and will be overcome. They should focus on the victories, no matter how small they seem. And they should be confident that substantial growth can and will be achieved.

This attitude of positivity, writes the Rebbe, is wholly necessary. It is a "precondition" for success. And it is not just necessary for the teacher or social worker. It is crucial for the person who is being worked with as well.

"Just as the said approach is important from the viewpoint of and for the worker and educator, so it is important that the trainees themselves should be encouraged both by word and the manner of their training to feel confident that they are not, G-d forbid, 'cases,' much less unfortunate or hopeless cases, but that their difficulty is considered, as above, only temporary, and that with a concerted effort of instructor and trainee the desired improvement could be speeded and enhanced."

The Rebbe also emphasizes the need for caregivers to feel and exude optimism, for the residents of the group home to be given leadership roles within the home, and for the Jewish needs of the residents to be consciously focused on, attended to, and nurtured.

The Rebbe concludes his reply by referencing a line in Dr. Wilkes' letter, where the latter praises the Rebbe and the Chabad-Lubavitch movement for having "deep concern for every Jewish individual's welfare." The Rebbe refers to this line, and remarks:

"Needless to say, such appreciation is very gratifying, but I must confess and emphasize that this is not an original Lubavitch idea, for it is basic to Torah Judaism. Thus, our Sages of old declared that ve'ohavto lere'acho ko'mo-cho ('Love your fellow as yourself') is the Great Principle of our Torah, with the accent on "as yourself," since every person surely has a very special, personal approach to himself. To the credit of the Lubavitch emissaries it may be said, however, that they are doing all they can to implement and live by this Golden Rule of the Torah, and doing it untiringly and enthusiastically."

This correspondence opens a new window into the Rebbe's revolutionary approach to inclusion—an approach that was, in the Rebbe's own view, the furthest thing from being revolutionary.

To the Rebbe, the biblical injunction to "Love your fellow as yourself" meant exactly that—*to love your fellow as you love yourself.* No hidden meanings, no allegories, no riddles. It's patently straightforward.

Who's included in "our fellow"? *Everyone.*

It is therefore inconceivable to exclude or disrespect another person for some perceived differences. Our mandate to love our fellow as ourselves means that we are to be there for the other, care for them, and actively seek out the best for them. We must love another with all their individuality—just as we love ourselves and our individuality.

The Rebbe saw this as a basic and fundamental Jewish value, not specific or exclusive to the Chabad-Lubavitch movement.

And yet, we might say that the *way* in which the Rebbe lived by and implemented this value of un-mitigated love for another was altogether unique.

The Rebbe built up the Chabad-Lubavitch move-ment from the ashes of the Holocaust into a global force of goodness and kindness. The Rebbe sent out thousands of emissaries, *shluchim*, to locations around the world. Often these emissaries would arrive in remote places devoid of Jewish infrastructure. Yet the task was always the same. Roll up your sleeves and get to work on caring for the needs of the Jews in that location.

The foundation of these efforts was, and still is, *love*. Love for another Jew. Love for someone you may have never met before, and may never meet again.

The Rebbe taught time and again: You must love your fellow as yourself! If you've discovered the beauty and richness of Judaism, share that gift with another. Encourage another person to study Torah, practice *mitzvot*, and bring beautiful G-dly light into this world. And always do it with love.

The Rebbe took the mitzvah to love another very seriously.

In the summer of 1994, five weeks after the Rebbe's passing, Rabbi Zev Segal, the longtime spiritual leader of Young Israel of Newark and one-time president of the Rabbinical Council of America, delivered a tribute to the Rebbe. In his tribute, Rabbi Segal emphasized the magnitude of the Rebbe's global leadership.

"The leadership of world Jewry was given to the Lubavitcher Rebbe, and he fulfilled that mission to the maximum. The entire people of Israel were his concern, and a deep concern. Jews in every corner of the world, no matter how forsaken and no matter how small in number, were on his mind and in his heart and soul.

"If there was a man qualified to reconstruct Jewish life after the great 'Churban,' the tragic Holocaust that befell our people, it was the Rebbe. He reconstructed Jewish life, making Jews, without any exception, no matter what their station in life, feel that they are part of this reconstruction. He was concerned about every Jew wherever he was.

"This was a unique devotion and dedication to world Jewry."

The Rebbe, in his pure and essential love of every single Jew, personified the dictum of "Love your fellow as yourself."

Rabbi Jonathan Sacks, former chief rabbi of the United Hebrew Congregations of the Commonwealth, expressed the Rebbe's campaign to love every Jew in these terms.

"If the Nazis searched out every Jew in hate, we will search out every Jew in love."

And so, the Rebbe sent thousands of *shluchim* across the globe, to open Chabad Houses, schools, camps, senior centers, soup kitchens, and more. All with the same core mission: to search out every Jew, in love.

To the Rebbe, every Jew was family, every Jew had a home, every Jew was connected. This love guided the Rebbe's inspiring approach to inclusion.

When you love, you don't exclude others. When you love, you don't simply "tolerate" others. When you love, you don't simply "accommodate" others.

When you love, you include all—organically and naturally. In a way that makes the other feel loved and welcomed.

The Rebbe laid out this inclusionary approach in his correspondence with Dr. Wilkes in the summer of 1979. Exude positivity and joy, empower with leadership, and help nurture the Jewish connection.

And do this all from a place of love.

The famed Kabbalistic work *Reishit Chochmah*, authored by 16th century Israeli mystic Rabbi Eliyahu de Vidas, teaches us about the origins of love:

"Love emerges from contemplating how we were all formed by one Craftsman in His image, as it says, 'In the image of G-d, He created man'—if a person disgraces his friend, he discredits himself."

Love, then, stems from a place of unity—Divine unity and human unity. It therefore follows that it must lead back to unity, oneness, and inclusion, for all.

In 1976, Mrs. Chava Lehman founded a school for children with complex learning disabilities in London. She named the school Kisharon, which means "ability," "capacity," and "skill," since the school was founded upon the belief that every person has strengths and abilities that are a gift to themselves and the world.

Mrs. Lehman was inspired to open Kisharon in part due to the urging of Rebbetzin Amelie Jakobovits, the wife of then-chief rabbi of the United Hebrew Congregations of the Commonwealth Rabbi Immanuel Jakobovits. Rebbetzin Jakobovits told Mrs. Lehman: "Every Jewish child must be offered an education." In 1976, Mrs. Lehman opened Kisharon Day School.

Mrs. Lehman penned a letter to the Rebbe on June 8, 1982, in which she described her educational work.

One day later, the Rebbe replied:

"There is no need to emphasize to you at length that it is the duty of every Jew to do everything that he or she can to help other Jews, particularly special children who need special attention and care. Indeed, this is the elementary duty associated with the mitzvah of *V'Ahavta L'Reacha Kamocha* (love your fellow as yourself)."

To the Rebbe, the mandate to love our fellow imparted a personal obligation to ensure that every Jew is helped and cared for, and included.

Chapter Four

Individuality

"Everyone is obligated to say, 'It is for my sake that the world was created.'"

—Mishnah, Sanhedrin 4:5

J anuary 24, 1983. The Hebrew date is Yud Shevat, the tenth day of Shevat.

On this day in 1950, Rabbi Yosef Yitzchok Schneersohn, the Rebbe's revered father-in-law and predecessor, passed away. And on this day, exactly one year later, the Rebbe convened a farbrengen, a public gathering, and formally accepted the leadership of the Chabad-Lubavitch movement.

Every year since, on Yud Shevat, the Rebbe leads a far-brengen to mark this auspicious day.

The Rebbe's Yud Shevat farbrengens are legendary. Each year he delivers a new discourse that offers fresh insight into the final discourse published by his father-in-law, along with talks that energize and galvanize the

Chabad-Lubavitch movement. Each year people come from far and wide to be part of this uplifting experience.

On Yud Shevat in 1983, thousands of people pack the Rebbe's large basement synagogue in Brooklyn. The energy in the room is charged.

The Rebbe speaks for several hours, teaching, uplifting, inspiring, and challenging the assembled. The talks are punctuated by the singing of chasidic songs.

A major theme of the Rebbe's address this day is the rallying cry of his father-in-law that "America is not different." This is a declaration that Jewish values can and must thrive in a modern world. Jewish values and practice are not outdated or old-fashioned. Quite the contrary, Jewish values are needed today more than ever before. And, as the Rebbe points out, it is the responsibility of each one of us to ensure that Judaism thrives in our times.

At the midway point of the farbrengen *the Rebbe focuses his talk on the mitzvah to "Love your fellow as yourself." In the context of this* farbrengen, *this mitzvah can be understood as a scriptural basis for our mandate to help others grow Jewishly, and to ensure that spiritually, America is indeed not different. After all, if you truly love your fellow as yourself, you will see to it that they, too, have the opportunity to celebrate their rich heritage.*

During his talk, however, the Rebbe highlights another powerful element of this mitzvah.

*To love another as yourself does not mean that you give them what **you** need. To truly love another as yourself means that you give them what **they** need.*

Giving the other what you need is not true love at all. It's selfish love.

Giving the other what they need even when it's not at all what you need—even when it's the opposite of what you need—is a pure indication that your love for them is truly about them.

The Rebbe explains this by means of a simple example:

Imagine you are thirsty, while your fellow is hungry. Loving your fellow as yourself means that you give them a piece of bread—not that you give them water. Although water is what you need right now, it's not at all what they need.

"If, as a result of 'Love your fellow as yourself,'" says the Rebbe, "you who are thirsty take away all your friend's bread and instead give him a barrel filled with water, it is the opposite of 'Love your fellow as yourself'!

"True, this action is consistent with the ideal of treating another 'as yourself,' since you who are thirsty are giving him water. But to truly 'Love your fellow' you must pay

attention to what your fellow needs. And that might just be the opposite of what you need."

The Rebbe then connects this deeper understanding of the mitzvah with the theme of the farbrengen.

It is true that there is a spiritual manner by which to practice the mitzvah to "Love your fellow as yourself"—through teaching, guiding, and inspiring others Jewishly. And there is tremendous value and importance in this.

Yet, we must always remember that the most basic meaning of loving our fellow is to provide him or her with what they most immediately need—even if that is a basic, material need.

It is not enough to care about another person's spiritual wellbeing. We must also care about their physical wellbeing.

In the Rebbe's words: "When one encounters a person who asks simply for bread and water, and he responds, 'I'd like to teach you Torah, since I am a leader of your tribes and Torah study is the most important of all'— that is actually the opposite of charity! It is the opposite of the meaning of the commandment in the very Torah that you want to teach him!"

L ove, as the Rebbe points out, can be very tricky to navigate. Sometimes, love can become so distorted that it leads to actions that are not at all loving.

Love becomes distorted when we take only ourselves into account and fail to consider the other person's individuality.

When we project our wants and needs upon others, when we imagine that what *we* want is what *they* want, when we only consider ourselves and fail to consider their unique wants and needs, we are not, in fact, loving them—we are loving ourselves.

This is a self-oriented, self-reflective love. Not a giving love.

A true, giving love is always a selfless love.

True love values the other *as they are*. True love honors the other's individuality and personality. True love means that we recognize that every person is a unique individual with different wants and needs.

True love is never about us. It's always about the other.

So if you need water but your friend needs bread, then truly loving them means to give them *bread*— even though that's not at all what you need.

And if your friend has a pressing, practical, physical need, then true love demands that you help them with that need. It's not the appropriate time to provide for their spiritual needs—even if that is what is most important to you.

⌁

The Rebbe's message about selfless, individualized love and care is at the heart of inclusion.

Inclusion means that we love, honor, and respect the person as they are, wholly and completely. Inclusion means that we embrace the other as a unique individual, with unique loves, fears, hopes, dreams, wants, and needs.

In his letter to Dr. Wilkes in August 1979, responding to the question of which setting would be most appropriate for Jewish individuals with intellectual disabilities, the Rebbe writes:

"With regard to the efforts which have been made in recent years to create 'group homes'... which, as you say, has been a source of controversy, it is to be expected that, as in most things in our imperfect world, there are pros and cons. However, I believe that the approach should be the same as in the case of all pupils or students who spend part of their time in group environments: school, dormitory, summer camp, etc., and part of their time in the midst of their families, whether every day, or at weekends, etc. Only by individual approach and evaluation can it be determined which individual fits into which category."

The Rebbe was careful not to offer a one-size-fits-all response to Dr. Wilkes' question. Instead, the Rebbe highlighted that each person is an individual, with individual needs. Therefore, the only valid manner by which to determine the best setting for the growth of an individual is on a person-by-person basis.

❦

The idea that human beings are to be regarded as individual and unique, and not simply as a nameless, faceless mass of humanity, is among the most classic and powerful Jewish teachings.

History is replete with societies that sought to devalue and dehumanize the individual. The only thing that was important, according to this worldview, was the community as a whole. It was therefore right and just for the individual to be sacrificed, both figuratively and literally, for the good of the people.

Judaism categorically rejects this notion.

Judaism teaches that the human being—every human being—possesses infinite value as an *individual.*

G-d created the first human as a single being, our tradition teaches us, to hammer home this very point—that every single human being has infinite value.

The Sages of the Talmud articulated this Jewish belief in the value of the individual when they likened each and every human being to an entire world (*Sanhedrin* 37a):

"Whoever destroys a soul, it is considered as if he destroyed an entire world. And whoever saves a life, it is considered as if he saved an entire world."

A human being—*every* human being—is an entire world. And no two worlds are alike.

The Mishnah says as much when extolling the greatness of G-d in creating diversity among human beings. Considering that the Torah tells us that the human being is created in the "image of G-d," the Mishnah exclaims (ibid. 38a):

"This is the greatness of the Holy One, blessed be He. If a man strikes many coins from one mold, they all resemble one another. But the supreme King of kings, the Holy One, blessed be He, fashioned every man in the stamp of the first man, and yet not one of them resembles his fellow!"

The One G-d—perfect, singular, and indivisible— created many distinct and unique individuals. Each carrying G-d's image in his or her unique way.

This, the Chasidic masters say, evokes divine beauty, and a sense of G-d's majesty.

Human beings are unique individuals. We are not one-size-fits-all.

"Rabbi Meir would say: One person is different from another in three ways: In voice, in appearance, and in thought" (ibid.).

We don't sound the same. We don't look the same. We don't think the same.

And this is a good thing. It's a *blessing*.

Jewish law, in fact, prescribes an actual blessing to be recited when beholding a large group of people. As the Talmud teaches (*Berachot* 58a):

"One who sees multitudes of Israel recites, 'Blessed [are You, L-rd our G-d, King of the universe,] Who knows all secrets.' Why is this? He sees a whole nation whose minds are unlike each other and whose faces are unlike each other, and He Who knows all secrets—G-d—knows what is in each of their hearts."

Diversity and individuality is a blessing. It is a blessing that we think different and look different. G-d endeavored to create us in such a way that each of us should, in fact, be different. G-d did this because individuality is a blessing.

Therefore, when we encounter a manifestation of Divinely-ordained human diversity, it is only appropriate to recite a blessing.

The Chasidic masters further emphasize that every single individual has a specific role in completing G-d's master plan for creation. We are all here to be "partners in creation" and make the world a better place. And every individual does it in their own unique way.

"'You are My witnesses,' says G-d" (Isaiah 43:10).

Each one of us.

Individually.

Bearing witness to G-d.

In our own way.

If every human being possesses infinite value, if every human being possesses a Divinely-ordained uniqueness, if G-d desires human individuality, if every one of us plays a unique, individual, and irreplaceable role in the master plan of creation, then certainly we are to honor the uniqueness and individuality of every human being.

Infinitely.

Practically, as parents, teachers, family, friends, and community members, we must always be conscious to relate to others as individuals, and value and nurture their unique qualities.

And when we genuinely love, value, and appreciate the other person for who they are—this leads to true inclusion.

Chapter Five

Dignity

"G-d created man in His image;
in the image of G-d He created him."
—*Genesis 1:27*

The Rebbe has coined the Hebrew year 5750—stretching from late September 1989 to mid-September 1990—as "The Year of Miracles." It's a year to look beyond the ordinary, says the Rebbe, and see the extraordinary. To see the Divine majesty woven throughout all of existence. To behold the daily miracles happening before our very eyes.

"The miracles are here," says the Rebbe. "Open your eyes."

This theme pervades the Rebbe's communications this year, both in his public and private correspondences.

Six days before his eighty-ninth birthday, on a chilly March morning in 1990, the Rebbe addresses a very *human miracle: the profound dignity and infinite value of every single Jew.*

In a powerful talk combining dozens of sources from scripture, Talmud, Jewish law, philosophy, and Jewish mysticism, the Rebbe methodically builds the case that every single Jew—without exception—possesses im-measurable inner value.

"Every Jew—man, woman, or child—irrespective of where and how they live, is a Jew, a part of G-d's people, about whom G-d says, 'I have formed this people for Myself; they shall relate My praise.'"

The Rebbe emphasizes that the very existence of the Jew, by virtue of who he or she is—and not by virtue of what he or she does—is a treasured part of G-d's people.

"Therefore, we must take extreme caution to only bestow honor and dignity upon another person, and not to speak disparagingly about the other, G-d forbid...

"Indeed, one ought to be afraid of speaking negatively about a child of G-d..."

In that 1990 address, the Rebbe was speaking about a *miracle*—the miracle that lies within the heart and soul of every human being. The miracle that grants every person infinite inner worth.

The miracle of dignity.

The Rebbe saw human beings as gifted with not just human dignity, but with Divine dignity, carrying a soul that is, literally, a piece of G-d. An infinite piece of G-d in a finite body. This conjoining of heaven and earth is the ultimate miracle. And the ultimate source of dignity.

When you see human beings for who they truly are at their essence, and when you know that G-d honors and dignifies every person, you can't help but feel an acute sense of awe and respect toward another.

This magnificent teaching from the Rebbe high-lights the danger in sizing up others based on what we sense they can or cannot do. In that moment of judgment, we are commoditizing them, denying their Divine imprint, and robbing them of their true, infinite value.

⬥

The Talmud, the great repository of Jewish legal analysis and discourse, also contains many stories. Here is one curious Talmudic tale, from Tractate *Taanit* (20a-b), which touches upon the theme of human difference and dignity.

"Once, Rabbi Elazar son of Rabbi Shimon was coming from Migdal Gedor, from the house of his teacher. He rode along the riverside on his donkey and felt happy and proud because he had studied much Torah.

"He chanced upon an exceedingly ugly man, who greeted him, 'Peace be upon you, my master!'

"Rabbi Elazar did not return his greeting but instead said to him, 'Empty one! How ugly you are! Are all the people of your city as ugly as you?'

"'I do not know,' said the man. 'But go to the Craftsman Who made me, and say to Him, "How ugly is the vessel that You have made!"'

"Realizing that he had done wrong, Rabbi Elazar dismounted from his donkey, prostrated himself before the man, and said to him, 'I misspoke. Forgive me!'

"But the man replied, 'I will not forgive you until you go to the Craftsman Who made me and say to Him, "How ugly is the vessel that You have made."'

"Rabbi Elazar kept walking after him until he reached his city. The residents of the city came out to greet him, saying, 'Peace be upon you, O teacher! O master!'

"'Who are you calling master?' the man asked them.

"'The person walking behind you,' they replied

"'If this is a "master,"' said the man, 'may there not be any more like him in Israel.'

"'Why?' asked the people.

"'He has done such and such to me,' said the man.

"'Nevertheless, forgive him,' said they, 'for he is a man greatly learned in the Torah.'

"'For your sakes I will forgive him,' said the man, 'but only if he does not act this way anymore.'"

This Talmudic story is poignant and demanding. It demands of us that we answer, honestly, a fundamental personal question:

When we look at another person, what exactly do we see? Do we see the person's physical form, their body, their face? Or do we see the Divine Craftsman Who formed them?

How we answer this question has far-reaching ramifications.

If we size up another based solely on their perceived physical attributes, then we deny them their true dignity. And, as in the Talmudic story, that can very well lead to behavior on our part that is insensitive and hurtful.

If, however, we see another in their truest Divine form, made by the Divine Craftsman, then we are awed and humbled by their inner majesty. And we treat them with the utmost respect.

Rabbi Elazar saw the man as ugly.

The man reminded Rabbi Elazar that he bears the imprint of G-d.

The Talmudic narrative emphasizes just how hurtful and devastating our words are when we are lacking the proper dignity and respect for the other.

The Rebbe's 1990 address emphasizes just how healing and caring our words will be when we are filled with a deep sense of the other's true essence.

This carries a poignant message:

See others for who they truly are, recognize their inner Divine dignity, and you will relate to them in a healthy and dignified manner.

Seeing others as possessing infinite, Divine dignity affects not only our words, but certainly our actions as well. The Rebbe modeled this approach in behavior.

As a rule, when praying in the small, upstairs synagogue in 770—where he faced the congregation—the Rebbe tried to keep his face somewhat hidden. Perhaps it was to enable him to focus more intently on his own prayers. Perhaps it was to make sure that the Chasidim were not looking at him instead of attending to their own prayers. Whatever the case, it was obvious to all that the Rebbe quite intentionally covered his face during prayers.

But something different happened every time Shimon Fahima prayed in that synagogue.

Shimon was born with Klippel-Trenaunay syndrome, a rare congenital disorder that resulted in his face having a port-wine stain birthmark and an overgrowth of his mouth and lips. People, perhaps due to their discomfort or embarrassment, often went to great lengths to avoid looking at him.

From time to time Shimon would travel from his home in Israel to Crown Heights, where he would go to 770 and pray in the Rebbe's synagogue. When Shimon prayed in the Rebbe's congregation, the Rebbe made certain not to cover his face. He did not want Shimon, or anyone else present, to think that he found it distasteful to look at him. Shimon was very aware of this change in the Rebbe's behavior, and he treasured the dignity and respect that the Rebbe showed him.

If every human being bears G-d's signature and possesses infinite, Divine dignity, then we must act toward all with dignity and respect, never hurting another or compromising their feelings.

Indeed, this is one of the reasons why the Torah makes a point to tell us that human beings are created in the image of G-d—so that we recognize the inherent value of each and every person and grant them honor and respect.

In the words of the great sage Rabbi Akiva in *Ethics of Our Fathers* (3:14):

"Beloved is man, for he was created in the image [of G-d]. It is a sign of even greater love that it has been made known to him that he was created in the image [of G-d], as it is says, 'For in the image of G-d, He made man' (Genesis 9:6)."

It's one thing to be created in G-d's image. It's quite another to be *informed* of this.

Being told that we are created in the image of G-d is an act of *greater Divine love*, because it is with that knowledge that we may truly treat all human beings with the respect and dignity they deserve.

We must always act respectfully toward others and honor their Divine image, as 19th century scholar Rabbi Yisroel Lifschitz writes in his commentary on this teaching of Rabbi Akiva (*Tiferet Yisrael, Avot* 3):

"For this reason, one should act benevolently toward all, including someone who is not a member of the covenant. Certainly, one may not cause others harm, whether to their body, their wealth, or their dignity. One may not denigrate others, causing to blanch the image of G-d that shines from their face."

The message is clear: We must always relate to others with respect and sensitivity.

A nother profound demonstration of the Rebbe's sensitivity and his efforts to preserve the dignity of others occurred on a Shabbat in the summer of 1985.

No one noticed the group of visitors who had come to 770 for the first time that Shabbat. And that's exactly the way the Rebbe wanted it.

The date was June 1, 1985. Rabbi Sholom Ber Lipskar, spiritual leader of The Shul of Bal Harbor, had brought the group of twenty men to Crown Heights. A highlight of their visit would be taking part in the Rebbe's Shabbat farbrengen, *a public gathering where the Rebbe would share words of Torah and inspiration.*

But these were no ordinary guests.

Rabbi Lipskar also serves as the executive director of the Aleph Institute, an organization dedicated to serving the religious needs of Jewish men and women in prison and in the military. And on that Shabbat, he had brought twenty men who were prisoners in the federal prison system.

The Aleph Institute had struck an agreement with the Federal Bureau of Prisons in Washington, DC, to arrange a two-week furlough in Crown Heights for prisoners who met certain criteria. They would enjoy an immersive experience of Jewish study, prayer, and practice, and have the opportunity to participate in a farbrengen *with the Rebbe.*

Thousands of people crowded into the large synagogue that Shabbat afternoon. The farbrengen *was set to begin at its usual time of 1:30 pm. But shortly before the starting time, Rabbi Leibel Groner, the Rebbe's secretary who would typically accompany the Rebbe into the synagogue, came looking for Rabbi Lipskar.*

Rabbi Lipskar, who was at the opposite end of the syn-agogue, made his way through the enormous crowd to speak with Rabbi Groner.

Rabbi Groner told him that the Rebbe had suggested that the prisoners not be seated together at the farbrengen. *Doing so might evoke the curiosity of others and lead them to be asked who they were and where they came from. Having to identify themselves as federal prisoners might cause them embarrassment.*

Instead, the Rebbe said, they should be interspersed among the farbrengen *crowd. That would allow them to blend in and avoid embarrassment.*

The Rebbe cared deeply about the dignity of those twenty Jews who came to 770 that Shabbat, and he sought to preserve their self-respect.

In fact, the subject of one of his talks that afternoon was about the need to reform the prison system in order to preserve a prisoner's sense of dignity and humanity while incarcerated.

"Here was a leader who cared about a Jew in jail," says Rabbi Lipskar when reflecting on this story. "He was a leader who took every precaution not to even bring any sense of embarrassment to a person in jail."

The prisoners were astounded by this degree of care. As Rabbi Lipskar relates, "They were totally impacted;

they could not believe they were in the presence of such a person."

This is yet another example set for us by the Rebbe, teaching us how to relate to others with the utmost sensitivity, dignity, and respect.

This is true for the way we act toward others. And it's true for the way we talk about and to others.

*I*n the course of the correspondence between the Rebbe and Dr. Robert Wilkes, the Jewish social worker and community advocate for people with intellectual and other developmental disabilities, the latter invites the Rebbe to address a conference being planned in New York "on issues and needs of the Jewish retarded."*

Dr. Wilkes' letter is dated August 12, 1980, and he discloses that the objective of this conference is to discuss "how to make all aspects of Jewish living (e.g., education, community living, recreation, worship) available to the developmentally disabled individual and his/her family."

The Rebbe replies with a letter dated November 17, 1980, and includes remarks addressed to the conference, scheduled to take place the following month. In these remarks, the Rebbe speaks at length on the theme of Jewish education.

But it's what is mentioned almost in passing that causes one to sit up and take notice.

Referring to the use of the term "retarded" in the conference name, the Rebbe writes:

"Parenthetically, I prefer some such term as 'special' people, not simply as a euphemism, but because it would more accurately reflect their situation, especially in view of the fact that in many cases the retardation is limited to the capacity to absorb and assimilate knowledge, while in other areas they may be quite normal or even above average."

The Rebbe was encouraging Dr. Wilkes and the conference participants to avoid using disparaging labels and terms when referring to people with intellectual disabilities, and instead to use sensitive and uplifting terms.

Looking closely at the Rebbe's suggestion, the term he offers as an alternative is "special." This is not the same as the more popular term "special needs."

"Special needs," though more dignified than the alternative, still focuses on what a person is missing or lacking.

"Special" focuses instead on what a person possesses—the Divine image, human dignity, and unique gifts.

In this parenthetical note, the Rebbe teaches us that words are powerful, and that language matters.

Instead of focusing on the outside and labeling the other by what we deem them to be "missing," we ought to focus on the inside and describe them by their inner, dignified truth.

The words we use to describe another person don't simply reflect the way *we* think and feel about them. The words we use can have a real and tangible effect on *them*.

The Talmud expresses the power of our words with a cautionary teaching about the dangers of *lashon hara*, speaking ill about another (*Arachin* 15b):

"Negative talk kills three: the speaker, the listener, and the one being spoken about."

It's understandable that the speaker and listener are adversely affected by the negative talk. Participating in a negative conversation, in whatever capacity, indicates a lack of sensitivity toward the third party, and signals the "death" of a certain measure of one's own dignity.

But why does negative talk affect the person *being spoken about*?

It's because our words matter. As the Rebbe explains, our words create realities far beyond what we can perceive with our finite senses. Our words may appear harmless and benign to us, but in truth, our words are powerful beyond measure.

This is true in a spiritual, cosmic sense, as illustrated in the following story regarding the Baal Shem Tov, the founder of the Chasidic movement:

"A resident of Mezhibuzh had a quarrel with another. Once, while in the Baal Shem Tov's synagogue, he shouted that he would tear the other fellow to pieces like a fish.

"The Baal Shem Tov told his pupils to hold one another's hands, and to stand near him with their eyes closed. Then he placed his holy hands on the shoulders of the two disciples next to him. Suddenly the disciples began shouting in great terror: They had seen that fellow actually tearing his disputant like a fish" (*Hayom Yom*, 29 Tishrei).

Our words can also have a tangible, physical effect

on others. When we operate out of a lack of respect for another and speak about a person in a way that is insensitive or hurtful, it can have a practical negative effect on them.

As the Talmud teaches (*Arachin*, ibid.), "Death and life are in the hands of the tongue."

Words matter. And so does our sense of respect and dignity toward others.

The Rebbe consistently advocated for the dignity and inclusion of others who might have otherwise been marginalized and excluded. This advocacy is expressed beautifully in the Rebbe's approach to the question of whether or not guide dogs should be allowed in synagogues.

From 1927 to 1983, Polish-born Israeli Rabbi Menachem Mendel Kasher publishes thirty-eight volumes of an encyclopedic work on the Torah and Jewish law entitled Torah Sheleimah.

In a footnote in Volume 15 of this work, Rabbi Kasher cites his own ruling that a vision-impaired person may not bring a guide dog into a synagogue. He bases this on the biblical prohibition against bringing an animal received in exchange for a dog as a sacrifice in the Holy Temple. If an animal received in exchange for a dog is banned from entering a holy space, he reasons, certainly a dog itself would be prohibited.

In a letter addressed to Rabbi Kasher dated June 29, 1959, and in another letter to Rabbi Kasher dated July 22, 1959, the Rebbe advocates for a different position.

The Rebbe cites another great Jewish legal authority, Rabbi Moshe Feinstein, who just a few years prior had ruled that it was indeed permitted to bring a guide dog into a synagogue. And he presents counterarguments to Rabbi Kasher's legal proofs as to the inadmissibility of a dog into a holy place of worship.

But it's the way the Rebbe concludes his second letter to Rabbi Kasher that calls us to attention.

The Rebbe points to an unrelated ruling in the Code of Jewish Law that takes into consideration the pain and anguish someone might feel in being left out of synagogue, and argues that similar consideration ought to be given to a vision-impaired person who would be unable to attend synagogue without a guide dog.

"The point I am making here is... if it is important for him to attend synagogue, then we must obviously look for ways to enable this."

This is a powerful example of the Rebbe's pioneering

inclusionary approach, which stemmed in large measure due to his incredible appreciation of, and sensitivity toward, human dignity.

When we recognize the Divine dignity inherent in another human being, our natural approach will be one of inclusion. We will strive to ensure that no one feels left out or marginalized.

Chapter Six

Jewishness

"Educate a child according to his way; even when he grows old, he will not turn away from it."

—*Proverbs 22:6*

Cantor Joseph Malovany has dazzled audiences with his musical talents for almost his entire life.

As a young boy growing up in Tel Aviv, his parents notice his gifts and bring him to the Israel Conservatory of Music for an assessment. "You must give him a strong musical education," the heads of the Conservatory tell his parents. "It would be a sin not to."

So they do.

The Malovanys are poor. The family of five lives in a cramped, one-and-a-half bedroom apartment. There is no extra money, certainly not to purchase a piano. So Joseph's mother sells her wedding ring and uses that money to purchase a piano. Then they make space in their tiny home for the piano.

These are the humble beginnings of Cantor Malovany's illustrious musical career.

He studies under skilled musical instructors, practices piano religiously, and receives liturgic training from some of the great cantors in Tel Aviv.

By the age of nine he is leading a portion of the Friday night services in Tel Aviv's beautiful Bilu Synagogue. At twelve, he is conducting the High Holiday choir.

At nineteen, while still serving in the Israeli army, he is offered his first position outside of Israel: to be lead cantor at Yeoville Synagogue in Johannesburg, South Africa. When his army service is complete, he accepts the offer.

Cantor Malovany and his wife Beatrice have their first son, Zevi.

Zevi, they soon discover, is severely autistic.

Cantor Malovany is a dynamic and inspiring cantor, a generational talent, and soon he is offered the position of cantor at the prestigious Edgeware Synagogue in London, the largest synagogue in the British Isles. The Malovanys move to London in 1968.

In 1973, New York's famed Fifth Avenue Synagogue comes knocking. Enthralled by his beautiful spinto tenor voice, they want him to be their chief cantor. He accepts their offer, and the Malovanys move to New York City.

But Zevi remains in London.

Zevi is receiving specialized care in a Jewish institution geared for people with developmental disabilities. His parents feel that it will be best for him if he stays in London. With a heavy heart, they keep him there.

The years go by. Cantor Malovany's fame and reputation grows. As one of the top cantors in the world, he is much sought-after, performing internationally in concerts and inspiring many tens of thousands of people with traditional Jewish song and liturgy.

Despite all of his professional success, Cantor Malovany's heart aches for Zevi. He and his wife visit Zevi regularly in London, and they are keenly aware of his condition. They seek a blessing for him.

In 1989, they get an opportunity to receive a blessing from the Rebbe.

Starting three years earlier, the Rebbe has opened a weekly receiving line to the public, known in Chabad circles simply as "Sunday Dollars." It is no longer feasible for the Rebbe to conduct sit-down sessions with everyone who would like to meet with him. So now, each Sunday, the Rebbe stands near his office and personally greets thousands of people from all walks of life—young and old, men, women, and children, Jew and gentile alike—and gives them a blessing and a dollar bill to give to charity.

At "Sunday Dollars" people have the opportunity to make a request from the Rebbe and receive a specialized blessing. Given the sheer size of the line and the number of people waiting to see the Rebbe, requests, understandably, must be brief.

On Sunday, December 10, 1989, Cantor Malovany, his wife Beatrice, and their younger son Ellis wait in line to spend a moment with the Rebbe.

The moment arrives.

The Rebbe begins by praising Cantor Malovany for using his gifted voice in the service of G-d, and in inspiring the hearts of the congregation. The conversation then turns to a more personal nature, with the Rebbe inquiring about Cantor Malovany's family.

After introducing his wife and younger son and receiving the Rebbe's blessings for them, Cantor Malovany asks for a blessing for his older son Zevi.

"We have another son, who, unfortunately, is not well. He is autistic. He needs a blessing."

The Rebbe responds by lovingly offering that although autistic people might experience challenges in interpersonal relationships, they can relate very closely to G-d

"While they're not busy with people, they're busy with G-d."

The Rebbe suggests that Zevi has a deep spiritual and Jewish connection. A connection that ought to be nurtured.

This rings true. Zevi has, after all, responded well to Jewish practices in the past. Cantor Malovany tells the Rebbe that Zevi has expressed excitement when being taught to recite a blessing over food, and he treasures his tzitzit.

"Does he have a tzedakah *box in his room?" the Rebbe asks.*

"No."

"You can put one in there. The facility won't mind—charity is something everyone allows. It will benefit him, and when people visit him, he'll remind them that they must give charity."

Cantor Malovany nods in agreement. He tells the Rebbe that he and his wife will be visiting Zevi in London soon. They will see to it that this happens.

Looking back, this would prove to be a transformational moment.

Two and a half years later, in June of 1991, Cantor Malovany and his wife are once again standing before the Rebbe at "Sunday Dollars." This time, they wish to share some good news.

Cantor Malovany recalls their previous conversation and tells the Rebbe that he has seen to it that Zevi has a tzedakah *box in his room.*

Zevi has responded positively to this and has experienced intellectual and developmental improvements. "He understands what he's told, he moves around more. He's a bit more responsive."

The Rebbe gives a dollar bill to Cantor Malovany. "Send this dollar to the administration and ask them to place it in the tzedakah *box in his room." Then he hands another dollar bill to Beatrice.*

"This is for your son."

There are some who perceive Judaism to be exclusive and exclusionary. They see a divide between scholar and layman, between so-called "religious" and "secular." From this way of looking at things, fragmentation within the Jewish community is an inevitability.

But the Rebbe saw a different reality.

The Rebbe fiercely endeavored throughout his four decades of leadership to erase this perceived divide and to heal and unify communities.

In essence, the Rebbe sought to realize the democratization of Judaism.

Jewish study and practice, the Rebbe taught, are not the exclusive domain of Torah scholars or the self-proclaimed "religious." Rather, they are the eternal birthright of every single Jew.

Without exception.

This radical approach to Judaism applies equally to people with intellectual and developmental disabilities. The Rebbe advocated that Jewish study and practice opportunities be afforded to all, irrespective of perceived ability.

Inclusion means not just that everyone has a place within the community, but that everyone has a place *Jewishly.*

In the Rebbe's conception, disability inclusion is not distinct and separate from Jewish inclusion. The two must go hand in hand.

It's no surprise, then, that the Rebbe's message to Cantor Malovany was that he should nurture his son's Jewish connection and teach him to be a Jewish ambassador, sharing his love and value of *mitzvot* with others.

This would not only positively affect Zevi's spiritual health, it would also improve his physical health.

Indeed, Zevi's overall situation improved as his Jewish connection became nurtured.

Just as the Rebbe had foretold to Dr. Wilkes ten years earlier.

Ten years prior to his first encounter with the Malovanys, in his August 1979 letter to Dr. Wilkes, the Rebbe articulated his position that the Jewish needs of people with intellectual and developmental disabilities must be tended to, through Jewish education and encouragement of mitzvah observance.

Doing so is not only consistent with the goal of Jewish inclusion, explained the Rebbe. It also greatly benefits the recipient, in real and tangible ways.

"There is surely no need to emphasize at length that, as in all cases involving Jews, their specific Jewish needs must be taken into account. This is particularly true in the case of retarded Jewish children, yet all too often disregarded. There is unfortunately a prevalent misconception that since you are dealing with retarded children, having more limited capabilities, they should not be 'burdened' with Jewish education on top of their general education, so as not to overtax them. In my opinion this is a fallacious and detrimental attitude, especially in light of what has been said above about the need to avoid impressing the child with his handicap. Be it remembered that a child coming from a Jewish home probably has brothers and sisters, or cousins and friends, who receive a Jewish education and are exposed to Jewish observances. Even in the American society, where observant Jews are not yet in the majority, there is always some measure of Jewish experience, or Jewish angle, in the child's background. Now therefore, if the retarded child sees or feels that he has been singled out and removed from that experience, or when he will eventually find out that he is Jewish, yet deprived of his Jewish identity and heritage, it is very likely to cause irreparable damage to him.

"On the other hand, if the child is involved in Jewish education and activities, and not in some general and peripheral way, but in a regular and **tangible** way, such as in the actual performance of *mitzvot*, customs and traditions, it would give him a sense of belonging and attachment, and a firm anchorage to hold on to, whether consciously or subconsciously. Eventually even a subconscious feeling of inner security would pass into the conscious state, especially if the teacher will endeavor to cultivate and fortify this feeling."

In his November 1980 letter written in conjunction with the Conference for the Jewish Community on Issues and Needs of Jewish Retarded, the Rebbe once again called for Jewish inclusion, and spelled out the practical benefits of such an approach.

"Jewish survival depends on the kind of education that develops and nourishes Jewish identity in the fullest measure. And this must surely be the highest priority of all communal services.

"With regard to Jewish retarded... the Jewish identity factor is even more important, not only per se but also for its therapeutic value. The actual practice of *mitzvot* in the everyday life provides a tangible way by which these special people of all ages can, despite their handicap, identify with their families and with other fellow Jews in their surroundings, and generally keep in touch with reality. Even if mentally they may not fully grasp the meaning of these rituals, subconsciously they are bound to feel at home in such an environment, and in many cases could participate in such activities also on the conscious level.

"To cite one striking example from actual experience during the Festival of Succos this year. As is well known, Lubavitch activists on this occasion reach out to many Jews with Lulov and Esrog, bringing to them the spirit of the Season of Our Rejoicing. This year being a year of Hakhel, I urged my followers to extend this activity as much as possible, to include also Nursing Homes and Senior Citizens' Hotels, as well as other institutions. I was asked, what should be the attitude and approach to persons who are senile or confused, etc. I replied—all the more reason to reach out to them in this tangible way. Well, the reports were profoundly gratifying. Doctors and nurses were astonished to see such a transformation: Persons who had spent countless days in silent immobility, deeply depressed and oblivious to everything around them, the moment they saw a young man walk in with a Lulav and Esrog in his hand suddenly displayed a lively interest, eagerly, grasped the proffered Mitzvah-objects, some of them reciting the blessings from memory, without prompting. The joy in their hearts shone through their faces, which had not known a smile all too long.

"One need not look for a mystical explanation of this

reaction. Understandably, the sight of something so tangible and clearly associated with the joy of Succos evidently touched and unlocked vivid recollections of experiences that had permeated them in earlier years.

"If there is much that can be done along these lines for adult and senior Jews in special situations, how much more so in regard to special children, when every additional benefit, however seemingly small, in their formative years will be compounded many times over as they grow older. In their case it is even more important to bear in mind that while they may be handicapped in their mental and intellectual capacity, and indeed because of it, every possible emphasis should be placed on the tangible and audio-visual aspects of Jewish education in terms of the actual practice of *mitzvot* and religious observances—as I have discussed this and related aspects at greater length in my correspondence with Dr. R. Wilkes of the Coney Island Hospital.

"There is surely no need to elaborate on all above to the participants in the Conference, whose Rabbinic, academic, and professional qualifications in the field of Jewish Education and social services makes them highly sensitive to the problems at hand. I hope and pray that the basic points herein made will serve as guidelines to focus attention on the cardinal issues, and that this Conference will, as mentioned earlier, mark a turning point in attitude, and even more importantly in action vis-a-vis Jewish Education, long overdue."

The implications of the Rebbe's call for Jewish inclusion are staggering and inspiring.

Jewish schools are to provide education to *all Jewish children.*

Synagogues are to accommodate *all Jews.*

Jewish community events and celebrations are to be open and accessible to *every Jew in the community.*

This, of course, raises all sorts of pragmatic concerns.

For a Jewish school to adequately educate all children, including those with intellectual and developmental disabilities, the school will require additional staffing, additional training, and modified facilities—all of which require additional funding.

The Rebbe anticipated these challenges and preempted them in his 1979 letter to Dr. Wilkes:

"I am, of course, aware of the arguments that may be put forth in regard to this idea, namely, that it would require additional funding, qualified personnel, etc., not readily available at present. To be sure, these are arguments that have a basis in fact as things now stand. However, the real problem is not so much the lack of resources as the prevailing attitude that considers the Jewish angle as of secondary importance, or less; consequently the effort to remedy the situation is commensurate, resulting in a self-fulfilling prophecy. The truth of the matter is that if the importance of it would be seen in its true light that it is an essential factor in the development of the retarded Jewish child, in addition to our elementary obligation to all Jewish children without exception, the results would be quite different."

In his public letters and in private correspondence, the Rebbe emphasized time and again that we must see to it that we tend to the Jewish needs of every single Jew, without exception. That we implement inclusive solutions that speak to the entire Jewish community.

Judaism must be made accessible for all Jews. Jewish inclusion is our most basic mandate as a people.

Epilogue

"The beginning is wedged into the end, and the end is wedged into the beginning."

—*Sefer Yetzirah*

We conclude where we began—in 1976, in the large basement synagogue in Crown Heights where the Rebbe is meeting with the group of wounded Israeli veterans.

Toward the conclusion of his talk, the Rebbe circles back to the theme of oneness:

"It is the Jewish custom that when two people meet… they take each other's hand, expressing the fact that they are one.

"This is alluded to, as well, in the Torah. When the Ten Commandments were given, five were engraved on one tablet and five on the other. And so, when two Jews shake hands, the five fingers of one person meet the five fingers of the other, and together they reflect the Ten

Commandments, and the Ten Utterances by which G-d created the world, and G-d's Divine Providence over every single individual, wherever they may be.

"Therefore, before we conclude, I would be honored if I could greet you individually and shake each of your hands."

❧

The Rebbe gave the call.

Now it's up to each of us to extend our hand in love, friendship, respect, dignity, and oneness, and take the hand of the other.

Five merging with five.

In perfect unity.

We must stretch out our hand and embrace every member of our communities to make them feel welcomed, loved, and at home.

It's truly our community.

Each and every one of us.

❧

Photos

*Selected photographs
of personalities and moments
mentioned in this book*

The Lubavitcher Rebbe, Rabbi Menachem M. Schneerson, greeting an Israeli war veteran in the synagogue of 770 Eastern Parkway on August 19, 1976

The Israeli delegation at the Toronto Paralympic Games in August 1976

The Lubavitcher Rebbe, Rabbi Menachem M. Schneerson,
addressing a large group of Israeli war veterans in the synagogue
of 770 Eastern Parkway on August 19, 1976

Mrs. Chana Sharfstein receiving a blessing and a dollar bill from the Lubavitcher Rebbe on August 5, 1990

*Cantor Joseph Malovany receiving a blessing and a dollar bill
from the Lubavitcher Rebbe on December 10, 1989*

*Professor Reuven Feuerstein
(1921–2014),
Founder and Chairman of
the Feuerstein Institute*

Exceptional Soldiers

*Address of the Lubavitcher Rebbe,
Rabbi Menachem Mendel Schneerson,
to a group of injured Israeli war veterans on
August 19, 1976.*

*Adapted from a translation originally published in N'Shei
Chabad Newsletter (Tishrei 5779)*

I will speak [Hebrew] with the Ashkenazic pronunciation, to which I am accustomed, but I hope that everyone will understand.

When Jews meet it is customary to begin with a blessing. The foremost blessing is the blessing of peace—hence the greeting, "*Shalom Aleichem*! Peace unto you!"

When Jews from several locations and countries meet, this is a cause for joy. This is especially the case when Jews from the Holy Land—"upon which G-d's Eyes are focused from the beginning of the year to the end of the year"[1]—meet with Jews who live, for the time being, in the diaspora. Notwithstanding being exiled from our land and living in the diaspora, the physical distance does not truly separate us. Despite being "scattered and dispersed among the nations,"[2] we remain "one people" through our "distinct laws"— the laws of Torah—given to us by the One G-d. This is what unites us all, underscoring our ability to lift ourselves above the limitation of place.

We are not distinct individuals who are meeting by chance. Quite the contrary: We are one unified body, one people, who happen to be dispersed. And when we meet, the truth is revealed—that we are indeed

---

1 Deuteronomy 11:12.

2 Esther 3:8.

one people, despite being scattered in the diaspora or in different parts of the Holy Land.

Moreover, just as we can unite by rising above the confines of space, so too are we able to unite by transcending the limitations of time. This is the secret to the power and eternity of *Am Yisrael*, the Jewish nation. We are "the fewest among the nations"[3] only when considering a particular time and place. However, all Jews, from the experience at Sinai until the end of generations, are intertwined[4] to the point that we constitute one entity, one nation. Thus, we are numerous and powerful quantitatively as well.

Our ability to transcend the bounds of place and time stems from a Jew's innate ability to elevate the spiritual over the physical and quality over quantity. For this reason, despite being a minority, we did not agree to assimilate under any circumstances—even though it meant, at certain times in history, Jews giving up their lives. In prosperous times as well, when we were invited and pressured to remove the distinguishing barriers by adopting the lifestyle of our non-Jewish neighbors, we steadfastly held to the principle that we are a unique and special people. Even though we were a minority, we

---

3 Deuteronomy 7:7.

4 Based on the Talmudic phrase (*Shavuot* 39a) "*Areivim zeh bazeh.*"

elevated quality over quantity, thus imbuing our quantity with the strength of our quality.

This brings us to the next point:

When, for some reason, a person is lacking in something quantitatively, it is no reason at all to be dejected, G-d forbid. Quite the contrary: Since he is lacking something physically—by no fault of his own, or through doing a good deed, and especially through sacrificing himself in defense of the Jewish people in a particular place, and particularly in the Holy Land—this is proof positive that the Creator has endowed him or her with unique spiritual abilities. These abilities enable him or her to overcome that which ordinary eyes perceive as a physical, bodily deficiency, and shows that, in fact, this person is not just equal to all those around him, but moreover, he possesses an additional spirit that allows him to overcome the apparent physical shortcoming.

It is for this reason that I disapprove of the term "handicapped" being used for anyone, as this suggests some type of inferiority. On the contrary, we must emphasize that he is unique and exceptional, possessing unique abilities granted by the Creator, above and beyond the capacity of others. This enables him to overcome hardships and obstacles that others cannot overcome.

Therefore, in keeping with the "Jewish custom" to offer advice even in areas that are not one's business, I would like to suggest that the name be changed from "the disabled (*petzu'im*) of Israel" to the "exceptional (*metzuyanim*) of Israel"—whether exceptional by cause of war, or otherwise. This term also calls to mind the teaching of our Sages that when our ancestors were exiled in Egypt, "they were distinctive (*metzuyanim*) there."[5]

This is not merely semantics; rather, it describes the situation in the truest way. The very name highlights their unique and outstanding qualities that give them the ability to be a living example. With joy and self-confidence, they demonstrate how every Jewish man and woman—regardless of their physical or bodily state—possesses a soul that is "an actual part of G-d above,"[6] and that this Divine soul ultimately overcomes the limitations of the body, with the body acting in alignment with the soul's directives.

The above underscores another fundamental area in Torah, especially as it is elucidated in the teachings of Chasidism. Because the Torah requires us to "serve G-d with joy,"[7] and our service of G-d

---

5 *Sifri*, *Ki Tavo* §31, quoted in Pesach Haggadah.

6 *Tanya*, beginning of ch. 2.

7 Psalms 100:2.

encompasses our entire lifetime, it follows that we are provided with the ability to be in a state of joy throughout our entire life. When a person encounters difficulties, it awakens within him hidden powers that surface and become active. This enables him to proceed with happiness—notwithstanding the obstacles— and fulfill his mission of increasing light, spirituality, and holiness in the world. Doing so spreads recognition of G-d in the world, and demonstrates that His commandments and way of life are accessible to everyone to be fulfilled in a joyful manner.

As mentioned above, a Jew has the ability to transcend the limitations of time and space. Nevertheless, the goal is to accomplish the above within the framework of time and space. The space in which we find ourselves is a place of prayer and Torah study. The present time is the conclusion of the month of Av when we mourn the destruction of the Temple, and we are approaching the month of Elul when we prepare for the coming year, may it be good for us and for all the Jewish people.

The Alter Rebbe[8] explains[9] that during the month of Elul, when each person is preparing himself to

---

8 Rabbi Schneur Zalman of Liadi (1745-1812), the founder of the Chabad movement.
9 *Likkutei Torah, Re'eh*, 32b.

merit a positive verdict for the coming year, G-d makes it easier and assists him. In the terminology of the Alter Rebbe, G-d makes Himself accessible like a king in the field. When the king is in his palace, entry to submit requests is very restricted. However, when the king goes out into the field, there is no need to gain permission from the various officers. Rather, each and every person can approach the king directly—regardless of how he is dressed—and the king receives him with a smiling countenance. The king patiently listens to his requests and ensures that they will be taken care of.

May it be G-d's will that just as the month of Av is concluding, similarly all aspects of "destruction" should cease. Through each individual illuminating his life with Torah and holiness and building his personal Holy Temple, this will hasten the conclusion of the exile and the redemption through Mashiach, who will build the Holy Temple. Until this happens, each and every one should be blessed with a good and sweet year.

In line with another Jewish "custom," I will conclude with a request, and I hope that every man and woman here will receive my request graciously. The recent incidents perpetrated by terrorists in Uganda and Istanbul—as well as prior and subsequent attacks—require of us to intensify practical measures of security, which is connected with intensified spiritual security. This is, first and foremost, connected with the mitzvah of *mezuzah*.

I request that on your return to the Holy Land, each of you check that your *mezuzot* are all kosher and in the proper position, so that the mitzvah will be fulfilled properly. I would consider it a great honor if you would accept a gift from me through my representatives in the Holy Land: If those present will leave their addresses, you will each be visited at home by my representatives in Israel who will assist in checking the *mezuzot* and affixing them to the doorposts. They will also bring additional *mezuzot* for those who need. The mitzvah of *mezuzah* will certainly elicit and reveal G-d's protection over every Jewish man and woman, wherever they may be. In the words of King David, "G-d will guard your going and coming, now and for all time."[10]

Since we began with one Jewish custom, let us conclude with another:

When two Jews meet, it is customary to extend one's hand. This highlights the difference between "the hands of Esau"[11] and the hands of the Children of Israel. The hands of Esau engage in war, terror,

---

10 Psalms 121:8.
11 Genesis 27:22.

destruction, and the like. Whereas when Jews meet, they take each other's hand, expressing the fact that they are united as one.

This is alluded to, as well, in the Torah. When the Ten Commandments were given, five were engraved on one tablet and five on the other. And so, when two Jews shake hands, the five fingers of one person meet the five fingers of the other, and together they reflect the Ten Commandments, and the Ten Utterances by which G-d created the world, and G-d's Divine Providence over every single individual, wherever they may be.

Therefore, before we conclude, I would be honored if I could greet you individually and shake each of your hands, with a *"Shalom Aleichem."*

May your return to the Holy Land be in a successful and auspicious time, as planned. May it also be a true *"aliyah"*— the term commonly used—to the Land of Israel, an ascent in every sense of the word, both in your personal lives and in your public activities. Finally, the ultimate blessing is that G-d fulfill His promise: "I shall set peace upon the Land",[12] as well as upon the entire world, in addition to the promises: "You will sleep securely, with no one to

---

12 Leviticus 26:6.

fear, and I will lead you with your heads held high."[13] May every man and woman here, among the entire Jewish people, merit very soon the true and complete redemption through our righteous Moshiach.

You should all be blessed with a good and sweet year, and may we all meet again soon, with the coming of Moshiach. Then, we will also be united with our fellow Jews who are scattered amongst the nations, for "a great multitude will return"[14] to the Holy Land, speedily and joyfully. At that time, "G-d will be King," in a calm and peaceful manner, and everlasting joy will reign.

I would also be honored to present each one of you with a dollar. I thank you in advance if you would donate it to charity when you return to the Holy Land.

May each and every one of you be blessed in all that you need, both materially and spiritually, and in the spirit of the mission of the eternal Jewish people (as discussed earlier)—to elevate the spiritual over the physical, form over matter, and the soul over the body. This will be the true victory for the Torah in the Land of Israel and throughout the entire world, when all nations of the world will recognize that we

---

13 Ibid. 26:6, 26:5, 26:13.
14 Jeremiah 31:7.

were justified in our struggle throughout the ages to preserve our existence and distinction. Despite our dispersion, we remained one nation, living by our one Torah, given to us by the true and One G-d.

With blessing and many thanks for the great honor you have given me through your visit. May it be G-d's will that you succeed many times over in bringing joy, light, and Judaism to every place you will visit in the diaspora and afterward in the Holy Land as well.

(Following the address, the Rebbe extended his hand to each guest with the greeting "Shalom Aleichem," and gave each one a dollar to give to charity. Before leaving, the Rebbe wished everyone a good and sweet year.)

Letters

*A collection of correspondence
primarily between the Lubavitcher Rebbe,
Rabbi Menachem M. Schneerson,
and Dr. Robert Wilkes on the pressing
need for inclusion within the Jewish
community, during the years 1979-1982*

*Please note that the letters that are available have been
reproduced below; there are a few additional letters
referenced in the correspondence that are not available.*

NEW YORK CITY HEALTH AND HOSPITALS CORPORATION

CONEY ISLAND HOSPITAL

2601 OCEAN PARKWAY • BROOKLYN, NEW YORK 11235 • 212-743-4100

Child Development Center

August 9, 1979

Rabbi Menachem Mendel Schneerson
Lubovitcher Rebbe
770 Eastern Parkway
Brooklyn, N.Y. 11213

Dear Rabbi Schneerson:

As a Jewish social worker and the chairman
of Region II Council For Mental Retardation
in Brooklyn, I would be most interested
in learning what your views are regarding
'the care and education of Jewish retarded
individuals'—those persons who, from birth, are
slow in thinking, speaking and learning.

For many years, the retarded individual,
especially the severely retarded, was placed
in a large, state-operated institution, often
quite a distance from the individual's home and
community. During the past few years, efforts
have been made to create "group homes" in all
our neighborhoods throughout the city so that
parents who cannot continue to care for their
retarded sons or daughters have the choice
of placing their child in a small, home-like
setting: situated either within or nearby the
individual's community.

This policy of creating "group homes" for
the retarded—Jewish as well as non-Jewish—has
been a source of controversy and often bitter
opposition pitting parent against parent,
neighbor against neighbor, and political
leaders against one another. The basis for
these heated discussions include predictions

about lowering the economic value of homes in a community; fear that retarded individuals will commit vandalism or, even worse, commit crimes; and that the retarded themselves will feel uncomfortable surrounded by normal people. On the other hand, parents of the retarded want their children to live in a safe and healthy environment.

How may we view this issue—that is, caring for individuals who have a disability which requires life-long care and supervision—from a Jewish perspective? As a concerned Jew, I care very much about our Jewish community: how we treat one another and how we conduct ourselves as human beings. I am particularly interested in your comments and opinions, because the Lubavitcher movement, with its deep concern for every _Jewish_ individual's welfare, has added a spiritual dimension—a spark—to _all_ our lives!

As a married man with—thank Gd—two beautiful, healthy children (ages 2 and 5), I am also aware that there has to be an equal concern for both the individual as well as for one's total community. The question is: how do we protect and safeguard all of our Jewish children—the retarded and the non-retarded—so that they can have the opportunity to grow, to develop, and to live 'Jewishly'?

I would also welcome the opportunity to discuss any of the above with you or your representatives. Thank you for your cooperation.

Respectfully yours,

Robert Wilkes

Robert Wilkes,
Assistant Program Director/
Chairman, Region 11 Council
For Mental Retardation
743-4100, ext. 610

RW/ma

RABBI MENACHEM M. SCHNEERSON
Lubavitch
770 Eastern Parkway
Brooklyn. N. Y. 11213
493-9250

מנחם מענדל שניאורסאהן
ליובאוויטש

770 איסטערן פארקוויי
ברוקלין, נ. י.

By the Grace of G-d
22 Av, 5739
Brooklyn, N. Y.

Mr. R. Wilkes, Asst. Program Director/
Chairman, Region 11 Council For Mental Retardation
Coney Island Hospital
2601 Ocean Parkway, Brooklyn, N.Y. 11235

Greeting and Blessing:

This is in reply to your letter of Aug. 9,
in which you ask for my views on "the care
and education of Jewish retarded children,"
outlining some of the problems connected
therewith and prevailing policies, etc.

I must, first of all, make one essential
observation, namely, that while the above
heading places all the retarded in one group,
it would be a gross fallacy to come up with
any rules to be applied to all of them as a
group. For if any child requires an individual
evaluation and approach in order to achieve
the utmost in his, or her, development, how
much more so in the case of the handicapped.

Since the above is so obvious, I assume that
you have in mind the most general guidelines,
with a wide range of flexibility allowing for
the necessary individual approach in each
case. All the more so, since, sad to say, our
present society is poorly equipped in terms of
manpower and financial resources to afford an
adequate personal approach to each handicapped
boy and girl. Even more regrettable is the
fact that little attention (at any rate little
in relation to the importance of the problem)

is given to this situation, and consequently little is done to mobilize more adequate resources to deal with the problem.

Now, with regard to general guidelines, I would suggest the following:

(1) The social worker, or teacher, and anyone dealing with retarded individuals should start from the basic premise that the retardation is in each case only a temporary handicap, and that in due course it could <u>certainly</u> be improved, and even improved substantially. This approach should be taken regardless of the pronouncements or prognosis of specialists in the field. The reason for this approach is, first of all, that it is a <u>pre</u>condition for greater success in dealing with the retarded. Besides, considering the enormous strides that have been made in medical science, human knowledge, methodology, and know how, there is <u>no</u> doubt that in this area, too, there will be far-reaching developments. Thus, the very confidence that such progress is in the realm of possibility will inspire greater enthusiasm in this work, and hopefully will also stimulate more intensive research.

(2) Just as the said approach is important from the viewpoint of and for the worker and educator, so it is important that the trainees themselves should be encouraged both by word and the manner of their training to feel confident that they are not, Gd forbid, "cases," much less unfortunate or hopeless cases, but that their difficulty is considered, as above, only temporary, and that with a concerted effort of instructor and trainee the desired improvement could be speeded and enhanced.

(3) Needless to say, care should be taken not to exaggerate expectations through far-fetched promises, for false hopes inevitably result in deep disenchantment, loss of credibility and other undesirable effects. However, a way can surely be found to avoid raising false hopes, yet giving guarded encouragement.

(4) As part of the above approach, which as far as I know has not been used before, is to involve (some of) the trainees in some form of leadership, such as captains of teams, group leaders, and the like, without arousing the jealousy of the others. The latter could be avoided by making such selections on the basis of seniority, special achievement, exemplary conduct, etc.

(5) With regard to the efforts which have been made in recent years to create "group homes" for retarded individuals, which, as you say, has been a source of controversy it is to be expected that, as in most things in our imperfect world, there are pros and cons. However, I believe that the approach should be the same as in the case of all pupils or students who spend part of their time in group environments: school, dormitory, summer camp, etc., and part of their time in the midst of their families, whether every day, or at weekends, etc. Only by individual approach and evaluation can it be determined which individual fits into which category.

(6) There is surely no need to emphasize at length that, as in all cases involving Jews, their specific Jewish needs must betaken into account. This is particularly true in the case of retarded Jewish children, yet all too often disregarded. There is unfortunately a prevalent misconception that since you are

dealing with retarded children, having more
limited capabilities, they should not be
"burdened" with Jewish education on top of
their general education, so as not to overtax
them. In my opinion this is a fallacious and
<u>detrimental</u> attitude, especially in light of
what has been said above about the need to
avoid impressing the child with his handicap.
Be it remembered that a child coming from
a Jewish home probably has brothers and
sisters, or cousins and friends, who receive
a Jewish education and are exposed to Jewish
observances. Even in the American society,
where observant Jews are not yet in the
majority, there is always some measure of
Jewish experience, or Jewish angle, in the
child's background. Now therefore, if the
retarded child sees or feels that he has been
singled out and removed from that experience,
or when he will eventually find out that he is
Jewish, yet deprived of his Jewish identity
and heritage, it is very likely to cause
irreparable damage to him.

On the other hand, if the child is involved
in Jewish education and activities, and not
in some general and peripheral way, but in
a regular and <u>tangible</u> way, such as in the
actual performance of Mitzvos, customs and
traditions, it would give him a sense of
belonging and attachment, and a firm anchorage
to hold on to, whether consciously or
subconsciously. Eventually even a subconscious
feeling of inner security would pass into the
conscious state, especially if the teacher
will endeavor to cultivate and fortify this
feeling.

I am, of course, aware of the arguments that
may be put forth in regard to this idea,
namely, that it would require additional

funding, qualified personnel, etc., not
readily available at present. To be sure,
these are arguments that have a basis in
fact as things now stand. However, the real
problem is not so much the lack of resources
as the prevailing attitude that considers
the Jewish angle as of secondary importance,
or less; consequently the effort to remedy
the situation is commensurate, resulting in
a self-fulfilling prophecy. The truth of
the matter is that if the importance of it
would be seen in its true light that it is an
essential factor in the development of the
retarded Jewish child, in addition to our
elementary obligation to all Jewish children
without exception, the results would be quite
different.

Perhaps all the aforesaid is not what you
had in mind in soliciting my views on "group
homes." Nevertheless, I was impelled to dwell
on the subject at some length, not only
because it had to be said, but also because
it may serve as a basis for solving the
controversy surrounding the creation of "group
homes" for those children who are presently
placed in an environment often quite distant
from the individual's home and community - to
paraphrase your statement.

Finally a concluding remark relating to your
laudatory reference to the Lubavitch movement,
"with its deep concern for _every_ Jewish
individual's welfare," etc.

Needless to say, such appreciation is very
gratifying, but I must confess and emphasize
that this is not an original Lubavitch idea,
for it is basic to Torah Judaism. Thus, our
Sages of old declared that ve'ohavto lere'acho
ko'mocho ("Love your fellow as yourself") is

the Great Principle of our Torah, with the accent on "as yourself," since every person surely has a very special, personal approach to himself. To the credit of the Lubavitch emissaries it may be said, however, that they are doing all they can to implement and live by this Golden Rule of the Torah, and doing it untiringly and enthusiastically.

May the <u>Zechus Horabbim</u>, the merit of the many who benefit from your sincere efforts to help them in their need, especially in your capacity as Regional Chairman of the Council For Mental Retardation, stand you in good stead to succeed in the fullest measure and stimulate your dedication for even greater achievements.

With esteem and blessing,

M. Schneerson

Note: There is a letter missing from Dr. Wilkes to the Rebbe dated September 19, 1979—as referenced in the following letter.

RABBI MENACHEM M. SCHNEERSON
Lubavitch
770 Eastern Parkway
Brooklyn. N. Y. 11213
493-9250

מנחם מענדל שניאורסאהן
ליובאוויטש

‏770 איסטערן פארקוויי
ברוקלין, נ. י.

By the Grace of G-d
13 Tishrei, 5740
Brooklyn, N. Y.

Dr. R. Wilkes, DSW
Chairman, Region 11 Council for Mental Retardation
Coney Island Hospital
Brooklyn, N. Y.

Greeting and Blessing:

Because of the intervening High Holidays, my
acknowledgment of your letter of Sept. 19th
has been somewhat delayed.

Of course you have my permission to
disseminate my letter, if it can serve a
useful purpose in promoting the cause of
education in general, and of the "special
children" in particular. Indeed, since
every child is special and deserves special
attention, how much more so those who are
"slower" that others.

However, if the letter is to be disseminated,
an important reservation must be added,
which though self evident to a person like
yourself, may not be self evident to others,
and therefore must be clearly stated to them,
hence was not mentioned in my letter to you.

It is that in all that has been said in regard
to Jewish children - it is first necessary
to clarify the requirement of the Halacha
in regards to these children - depending on
their age and their level of comprehension
to make sure that the facilities meet these

requirements in terms of Kashrus, Shabbos, Teffilin, etc.

To add a timely note a propos of the New Year, which is a "Seventh Year, a Year of Shemittah" (Sabbatical Year), and also began on the day of the holy Sabbath, the main characteristic of the Sabbath day is that it is a day of "delight" (<u>Oneg</u>) for young and old, as it is written, "You shall call the Sabbath a delight, "which, by extension, also characterizes the entire New Year.

Hence, if there are children and adults who, for whatever reason, are in a situation which precludes them from enjoying the "Sabbath" delight, it behooves anyone who becomes aware of this to do everything possible to enable them to participate in this delightful experience. The fact that the knowledge of the existing situation has reached certain organizations and individuals - and everything is by Divine Providence, is a further indication that they are in a position to act on this knowledge. Should there be any difficulties, even real ones and not exaggerated or imagined, it only means that they have been commensurate capacities to overcome them. For as with all Divine commandments, the obligation is given together with the capacity to carry it out.Thus, in the final analysis, it is largely a matter of personal will and determination.

With esteem and blessing
of Chag Someiach,

P.S.
I take the liberty of enclosing a copy of my

New Year message, in which the significance of
the New Year, 5740 as a "Year of Sabbath" is
more fully discussed.

P.P.S.
I note in the zerox copy of my letter, which
you enclosed with yours, that the word "yet"
- added by hand (P. 2, 8 line from bottom),
as well as the line underscoring the word
"<u>tangible</u>" (Beg. P. 3) does not appear clear.
No doubt this will be rectified in the other
copies.

RABBI MENACHEM M. SCHNEERSON
Lubavitch
770 Eastern Parkway
Brooklyn. N. Y. 11213
___
493-9250

מנחם מענדל שניאורסאהן
ליובאוויטש
___

770 איסטערן פּאַרקוויי
ברוקלין, נ. י.

By the Grace of G-d
2nd of Shevat, 5740
Brooklyn, N. Y.

Dr. R. Wilkes, DSW
Chairman, Region 11 Council for
Mental Retardation
Coney Island Hospital
2601 Ocean Pkway.
Brooklyn, N. Y. 11235

Greeting and Blessing:

Since our exchange of correspondence some
months ago, I have not heard from you.

I am interested to know if there have been
any developments in regard to the subject
matter of our correspondence, and, if so,
would appreciate your letting me know about
it.

With all good wishes, and
With blessing,

M. Schneerson

NEW YORK CITY HEALTH AND HOSPITALS CORPORATION

CONEY ISLAND HOSPITAL

2601 OCEAN PARKWAY • BROOKLYN, NEW YORK 11235 • 212-743-4100

Brooklyn Region 11 Council For
Mental Retardation

February 19, 1980

Rabbi Menachem M. Schneerson
770 Eastern Parkway
Brooklyn, N.Y. 11213

Dear Rabbi Schneerson:

In a rather short period of time (since
we last exchanged. letters) there have been
a number of exciting developments such as
additional services being created for the
Jewish retarded individual but-at the same
time - some new developments which may in the
long run prove detrimental to our objective
of giving "special" care to the needs of the
Jewish retardate and his/her family. Before
I list and explain some of these exciting
and positive developments as well as some of
the more ominous concerns, I want to let you
know that I did make the effort to write you
again but my letter probably never reached
you (attached is a copy of my letter dated
9/19/79). Although I have shown your statement
to many different people (Jewish as well
as non-Jewish), I have not sent it to any
publications because I wanted to first get
your written authorization.

A few weeks ago I received a call from
a columnist from the <u>Jewish Press</u> - who
I believe writes a weekly column called
"Challenge" - who wanted to publish your

letter (I forgot to ask him how he got hold of it). I informed him that, since I hadn't received your permission, he should first get in touch with you. Let me say this: by your letter appearing in the <u>Jewish Press</u>, which has a rather larger readership, it would give many families with handicapped children a tremendous feeling of comfort and support. And families with retarded children. need all the support they can get just to "keep going" from day to day!

What are some of the exciting new developments? Federation of Jewish Philanthropies has decided to expand, on a full-time basis, their religious/cultural program started by a young, dynamic, and very competent orthodox Rabbi (Martin Schloss) . Rabbi Schloss and his dedicated staff assist Jewish retarded men and women, many of whom are severely retarded, in Jewish living - e.g.) celebrating Chanukah by lighting the menorah singing Chanukah songs, learning how to cook special holiday dishes. To Rabbi Schloss' credit he includes in his activities not only the retarded individual but their families. His program was only a few weeks in existence when it spread like wild fire throughout the city that 'finally' there is a Rabbi who loves the retarded and who wants to give them an opportunity to <u>experience</u> Yiddishkeit.

At about the same time Rabbi Schloss was demonstrating the need for a religious program, three Jewish orthodox mothers of retarded children (Mrs. R. Feinerman, Mrs. P. Gaffney, Mrs. T. Stone) began to organize other orthodox mothers with retarded children. The response to their request for a meeting was overwhelming. They received hundreds of

phone calls from Jewish mothers throughout
the city and even from other states: all of
whom had one thing in common: the desire
to see our Jewish community to do more for
its developmentally handicapped children
(retarded, epileptic, cerebral palsy, brain
injured, autistic). They have had two or three
meetings. I have sent them some material
including your letter. What these mothers
find most frustrating and anguishing is that
they would like to see their children in a
"Yeshiva" learning Chanukah songs rather than
Christmas carols. Even more heartbreaking is
the fact that some prominent orthodox Rabbis
have publicly made extremely insensitive
remarks about the retarded.

Another positive development is that
Federation of Jewish Philanthropies (I have
had meetings with Rabbi I Trainin and Rabbi
S. Sharfman) will soon distribute a new
brochure that lists all of its services for
the Jewish retarded individual and his family.
For some time many Jewish families were under
the impression that Federation had nothing
to offer their developmentally handicapped
children. In addition, Rabbis Sharfman and
Trainin expressed interest in sponsoring a
major conference on the Jewish retarded child:
so that perhaps for the first time we can
publicly acknowledge that our Jewish community
has retarded children who need all of our
help.

What are some of the more ominous
developments? Throughout the city there
will be an increasing push to create small
community group homes for- the retarded.
There is a legal document referred to as
the "Willowbrook Consent Decree" which
stipulates that by 1981 a certain number

(in the thousands) of retarded individuals must be living in these community residences throughout New York City. It is a <u>good</u> decree because it will give many retarded people a chance to live, hopefully, like a human being.

In Brooklyn, where there are already about 35-40 group homes in operation, 47 more such residences (under the sponsorship of private, voluntary agencies) will be opening within a year. About 20 additional homes will be sponsored by the state -- in all likelihood, the state will care for the nonambulatory, multihandicapped individual. From what I have recently learned, neighborhoods such as Coney Island, Brighton Beach, Sheepshead Bay which have either none or very few community residences for the retarded will begin to feel rather heavy pressure to open community homes (usually from 8 - 10 residents per/home) in their respective areas.

What is ominous is the fact that whereas previously Jewish agencies could recruit Jewish client , the pressure to create more and more community residences within a .fixed time period has allowed state officials to "pre-select" which clients are to be chosen for any given residence . In other words, private, voluntary agencies are finding that, if they want to obtain funds to operate a community residence for the retarded, they must "accept" the clients chosen by the state authorities. I have attempted without success to call Sanford Solender, Executive Vice-President of Federation of Jewish Philanthropies, to alert him to this new development so that he can use whatever political connections he has available to him to express his concern that .Jewish agencies not be prevented from serving <u>primarily</u> Jewish

retarded individuals. Only Jewish agencies
have Kosher Kitchens in their community
residences.

There are so many things I want to write
about - I am afraid of turning this letter
into a lengthy essay. Another development
which is ominous but regretfully not new
is the fact that many Hebrew Day Schools
"test" children with I.Q. tests to determine
if this or that child has the intellectual
ability to be enrolled in their school. If
the answer is "no", then the parents have to
"shop" around for another Yeshiva - which may
also have a policy of testing children prior
to enrollment. Although I am not against
psychological tests if and only if they- are
utilized to help a teacher or a parent on how
to best approach a particular child who may
be experiencing difficulty in a subject, I
find it almost impossible to believe that our
Jewish community has adopted this practice of
selecting "who" will be exposed to Torah and
who will not. Perhaps the best word I can find
to describe my feelings about this practice
is "appalled." To my dismay, this practice is
.widespread and not easily changed. But I am
determined to do what I can to change it no
matter how long it takes.

Let me conclude this letter by informing
you that in the weeks ahead a number of
people such as Rabbi Schloss, orthodox Jewish
mothers, and other concerned individuals
are planning to get together to begin to
coordinate our efforts so that whatever we
do will have the maximum impact. I have been
very fortunate to have two very good friends
(who also happen to be my colleagues at Coney
Island Hospital), Dr. Rabbi) Benjamin Sharfman
and his son-in-law Dr (Rabbi) Gerald Schwartz,

both psychologists, who have inspired me to "move" the Jewish community always another step higher on the rungs of charity.

Your correspondence has been for me a great source of pride and honor: which has given me a greater sense of hope that one day <u>all</u> Jews will treat each other with respect and compassion. Please feel free to call me should you need additional information. If you would like to discuss anything in this letter in more detail, I would be available to meet with you or your representatives.

Let me take ·this opportunity to wish you and your family a very happy and healthy Purim.

Respectfully yours,

Robert Wilkes

Robert Wilkes, DSW
Chairman, Region 11
Council For Mental
Retardation

Enc.
RW/ma

Region 11 Council For Mental
Retardation

April 3, 1980

Rabbi Shmuel M. Butman
Jewish Press
338 - 3rd Avenue
Brooklyn; N.Y. 11215

Dear Rabbi Butman:

The reason I've waited this long to send
you the enclosed material including the
exchange of letters between Rabbi Menachem
Mendel Schneerson and myself is twofold: (a)
only recently received Rabbi Schneerson's
letter - dated 13 Tishrei - which gives me
permission to disseminate his correspondence;
and , (b) . just received the minutes from
Rabbi Isaac N. Trainin (Federation of Jewish
Philanthropies) which documents Federation's
decision

to sponsor a major conference <u>vis a vis</u>
the needs of the Jewish retarded and his/her
family in October/November 1980.

In some of the letters that I wrote I have
underlined these sentences which reflect the
essence of my thinking - my way of letting you
know what I would like you to emphasize. On
the other hand, where I prefer you <u>not</u> quote
me I have put sentences in [brackets].

Since Rabbi Schneerson's letter (dated 22 Av 9, 5739) is, to my knowledge, the only 'statement' issued on the subject of retardation by an *'outstanding Torah authority,' I would hope that the <u>Jewish Press</u> would give his words prominence the week your column gets published. Perhaps that week the <u>Jewish Press</u> can have an editorial which challenges the practice of testing preschool children for enrollment in Hebrew Day Schools. The paper can also list services (with telephone numbers and names of contact persons) available to families of retarded and developmentally disabled individuals.

In other words, I think our Jewish community has to recognize - yes - we want and need Jewish scholars - but, in the final analyses, what counts is that our people care about each other, respect each other, and appreciate each other's contribution irrespective of one's 'intelligence quotient'.

This is one issue - the love and care of Jewish handicapped children - that can bring <u>all</u> Jews together. I felt very reassured when Rabbi Schneerson in one of his letters explained that with every Divine obligation (mitzvah) there is the capacity to fulfill that obligation. There is no question that we will need not only "funds" but the energy and the will to modify our opinions, to think about issues which we may prefer not to deal with, and to tolerate honest differences of opinion.

I am convinced that if our Jewish community can provide for the education and the well-being of <u>all</u> of our children, we will merit the coming of the <u>Mishiach</u>.

Thank you for your cooperation.

Sincerely yours,

Robert Wilkes

Robert Wilkes, DSW
Chairman, Region 11
Council For Mental
Retardation

* I could not think of any other
phrase which could adequately describe or
characterize the Lubuvitche Rebbe. Although I
am not an orthodox Jew, I still feel a close
and warm attachment to Rabbi Schneerson.
Perhaps it is his deep and abiding caring for
<u>all</u> Jews that has given me (and I'm sure to
many others!) the inspiration and vigor to do
what I'm doing.

RW/ma

August 12, 1980

Rabbi Menachem M. Schneerson
Lubavitch
770 Eastern Parkway,
Brooklyn, New York 11213

Dear Rabbi Schneerson:

Rabbi Dr. Benjamin Sharfman, chairman of
Federation's prospective conference on issues
and needs of the Jewish retarded, has given
me the honor and privilege to invite you (and/
or your representatives) to address this
conference. The conference will be held, with
G-d's help, on December 10th (from 4 P.M.-
8 P.M.) and on December 11th (from 9 A.M.-4
P.M.).

What should be remarkable about this
conference is that not only will the
participants be discussing how to make all
aspects of Jewish living (e.g., education,
community living, recreation, worship)
available to the developmentally disabled
individual and his/her family but also the
participants, perhaps for the first time
for a "Jewish" conference, will represent
a very broad spectrum of Jewish communal,
educational, and religious organizations. As
of this date, the conference will be assisted
by such diverse groups as Agudath Israel of
America, Torah Umesorah-National Society for
Hebrew Day Schools, Board of Jewish Education
(a Federation agency), and the Association of
Orthodox Jewish Parent of the Retarded.

Since the conference's planning committee
is still putting the finishing touches
on the structure and scheduling of the
conference, official publicity material has

not been printed. Even the exact site for
the conference has not been printed. Even
the exact site for the conference has not
been printed. Even the exact site for the
conference has not been decided upon except
that it will be somewhere in Manhattan. Rabbi
Dr. Moshe Tendler has agreed to be the keynote
speaker on Wednesday, December 10th at 4:30
P.M. followed by a panel response. The core
of the conference will consist of workshops:
1) communal and professional attitudes, 2)
services needed, 3) Jewish identity and
education, and 4) funding for services and
facilities. The leaders or moderators of
these workshops will be Rabbis, educators,
social workers, parents of the retarded, and
administrators.

It is no secret that the Lubavitch
movement—perhaps more than any other Jewish
group—has emphasized the critical significance
of Jewish education for all Jewish boys
and girls as well as the overall need of
Yiddishkeit for all Jews. We would welcome
a statement from you prepared for this
occasion: to be read at the conference by
either yourself or by a representative. You
may also consider the possibility of sending a
specially prepared taped message. Please feel
free to consider any form of communication
which you think would be most meaningful.

The Reason why Rabbi Dr. Benjamin Sharfman
and I want so much to have you and/or your
emissaries involved with what we believe
will turn out to be a most stimulating and
challenging conference is not only because
Lubavitch's long-standing record of conducting
effective educational campaigns but also it
was your letter (which Rabbi Butman published
in its entirety in the June 20th issue of the

Jewish Press) which gave Dr. Sharfman and
myself (and Rabbi Sharfman's son-in-law Rabbi
Dr. Gerald Schwartz) the inspiration and
credibility to do all the necessary groundwork
that must be done to organize such a major
conference.

May I take this opportunity to once again
thank you for your continued interest and
support. You can feel free to respond to
either myself or to Dr. Sharman.

Wishing you and your entire family a very
happy and healthy New Year.

Respectfully yours,

Robert Wilkes

Robert Wilkes, DSW
Chairman, Brooklyn
Region 11 Council
For
The Retarded

cc.: Rabbi Dr. B. Sharman, c/o Child
Development Center at Coney Island
Hospital, 2061 Ocean Parkway, Brooklyn,
New York 11235

Rabbi Isaac Trainin, Director, Department
of Religious Affairs, Federation of Jewish
Philanthropies of New York, 130 East 59th
street, New York, N.Y. 10022

RABBI MENACHEM M. SCHNEERSON
Lubavitch
770 Eastern Parkway
Brooklyn. N. Y. 11213
493-9250

מנחם מענדל שניאורסאהן
ליובאוויטש

770 איסטערן פארקוויי
ברוקלין, נ. י.

By the Grace of G-d
9th of Kislev, 5741
Brooklyn, N. Y.

Dr. R. Wilkes, DSW
Chairman, Brooklyn
Region 11 Council for The Retarded
c/o Coney Island Hospital
2601 Ocean Parkway
Brooklyn, N. Y. 11235

Greeting and Blessing:

This is to acknowledge receipt of your
letter of Nov. 13th, with the enclosures in
connection with the forthcoming Conference.

Since the matter is of the greatest
importance, I have taken time out, despite
the pressure of duties, to respond with the
enclosed message. You can also supplement it
with my past correspondence with you on this
subject.

May Gd grant that every one of us should
do the utmost along the lines suggested in my
message, especially since we have the promise
of Divine aid in all such good efforts.

With esteem and
blessing

RABBI MENACHEM M. SCHNEERSON
Lubavitch
770 Eastern Parkway
Brooklyn, N. Y. 11213
493-9250

מנחם מענדל שניאורסאהן
ליובאוויטש

770 איסטערן פּאַרקוויי
ברוקלין, נ. י.

By the Grace of G-d
9 Kislev, 5741
Brooklyn, N. Y.

To All Participants in the
Major Conference for the Jewish Community
On Issues and Needs of Jewish Retarded
New York City.

Greeting and Blessing:

I was pleased to be informed of the
forthcoming Conference. I trust it will mark
a turning point in the attitude of community
leaders to Jewish education in general, and to
so-called Special Education in particular.

In any discussion relating to the wellbeing
of the Jewish community, the primary, indeed
pivotal, issue should surely be Jewish
Identity—that which truly unites our Jewish
people and gives us the strength to survive
and thrive in a most unnatural, alien, and all
too often hostile environment.

Historically—from the birth of our nation
to this day—Jewish identity, in the _fullest_
sense of this term, has been synonymous with
traditional Torah-Judaism as our way of life
in everyday living. Other factors commonly
associated with a national identity, such
as language, territory, dress, etc., could
not have played a decisive role in Jewish
survival, since these changed from time to
time and from place to place. The only factor

that has not changed throughout our long history has been the Torah and Mitzvos which are "our life and the length of our days." The same Tefillin, Tzitzis, Shabbos and Yom-Tov have been observed by Jews everywhere in all generations. Clearly there is no substitute for the Torah-way as the source and essence of our Jewish people.

Recognizing this *prima facie* fact, means recognizing that Jewish survival depends on the kind of education that develops and nourishes Jewish identity in the fullest measure. And this must surely be the highest priority of all communal services.

With regard to Jewish retarded—parenthetically, I prefer some such term as "special" people, not simply as a euphemism, but because it would more accurately reflect their situation, especially in view of the fact that in many cases the retardation is limited to the capacity to absorb and assimilate knowledge, while in other areas they may be quite normal or even above average—the Jewish identity factor is even more important, not only *per se* but also for its therapeutic value. The actual practice of Mitzvos in the everyday life provides a *tangible* way by which these special people of all ages can, despite their handicap, identify with their families and with other fellow Jews in their surroundings, and generally keep in touch with reality. Even if mentally they may not fully grasp the meaning of these rituals, subconsciously they are bound to feel at home in such an environment, and in many cases could participate in such activities also on the conscious level.

To cite one striking example from actual experience during the Festival of Succos this year. As is well known, Lubavitch activists on this occasion reach out to many Jews with Lulov and Esrog, bringing to them the spirit of the Season of Our Rejoicing. This year being a year of <u>Hakhel</u>, I urged my followers to extend this activity as much as possible, to include also Nursing Homes and Senior Citizens' Hotels, as well as other institutions. I was asked, what should be the attitude and approach to persons who are senile or confused, etc. I replied—all the more reason to reach out to them in this tangible way. Well, the reports were profoundly gratifying. Doctors and nurses were astonished to see such a transformation: Persons who had spent countless days in silent immobility, deeply depressed and oblivious to everything around them, the moment they saw a young man walk in with a Lulav and Esrog in his hand suddenly displayed a lively interest, eagerly, grasped the proffered Mitzvah-objects, some of them reciting the blessings from <u>memory</u>, without prompting. The joy in their hearts shone through their faces, which had not known a smile all too long.

One need not look for a mystical explanation of this reaction. Understandably, the sight of something so tangible and clearly associated with the joy of Succos evidently touched and unlocked vivid recollections of experiences that had permeated them in earlier years.

If there is much that can be done along these lines for adult and senior Jews in special situations, how much more so in regard to special children, when every additional benefit, however seemingly small, in their

formative years will be compounded many times
over as they grow older. In their case it is
even more important to bear in mind that while
they may be handicapped in their mental and
intellectual capacity, and indeed because of
it, every possible emphasis should be placed
on the tangible and audio-visual aspects
of Jewish education in terms of the actual
practice of Mitzvos and religious observances—
as I have discussed this and related aspects
at greater length in my correspondence with
Dr. R. Wilkes of the Coney Island Hospital.

There is surely no need to elaborate
on all above to the participants in the
Conference, whose Rabbinic, academic, and
professional qualifications in the field of
Jewish Education and social services makes
them highly sensitive to the problems at
hand. I hope and pray that the basic points
herein made will serve as guidelines to focus
attention on the cardinal issues, and that
this Conference will, as mentioned earlier,
mark a turning point in attitude, and even
more importantly in _action_ vis-a-vis Jewish
Education, long overdue. With prayerful wishes
for Hatzlocho, and with
                    esteem and blessing,

December 29, 1980

Rabbi Menachem M.Schneerson
770 Eastern Parkway
Brooklyn, N.Y 11213

    Dear Rabbi Schneerson:

    The conference (attended by about 250
persons) on "Serving The Jewish Retarded
Issues and Needs," sponsored by Federation of
Jewish Philanthropies, is over but our work
has really just begun. We will again meet
on January 15, 1981 to review what has been
accomplished and what we must do in the days
ahead.

    At the conclusion Of our conference, we
made a number of recommendations - a few of
them are:

    1. Federation has to sponsor more group
       homes (with Kosher Kitchens)for the
       retarded;

    2. Federation has to allocate more funds
       to all aspects of Jewish education
       including special education;

    3. We have to influence Hebrew Day Schools
       not to utilize I.Q. tests to disqualify
       children and thereby deprive them of a
       Jewish education;

    4. We have to support the UJA - Federation
       campaign since we cannot expect 'to
       take' without also 'giving.'

    5. We must continue to request the various
       Boards of Rabbis throughout the city

to issue proclamations in behalf of our
Jewish retarded and developmentally
handicapped.

It was a remarkable conference! I have not
had the opportunity to attend many Federation
conferences but I can say with pride that
for two days (Dec.10th and 11th) all the
participants - Jews from all walks of life
- spoke about the very same things you had
noted in your message: Torah, Mitzvahs and
Yiddeshkeit

Let me be candid. A few weeks prior to the
conference (I had informed Rabbi Groner) I
was greatly discouraged by the fact that some
orthodox groups, rather, abruptly, withdrew
their support: due to sharp differences in
religious perspectives (or principles).
I had no idea that our community was so
polarized: that various parties have such
little respect for each other's viewpoints.
Why is it so difficult for our religious
groups to accept their own philosophy and
practice while at the same time accept (and
respect) the contribution that another group
can make to Judaism? (I secretly thought that
this conference -at which time we all would
sit down together as a unified community -
would increase the sense of unity within our
community and thereby speed the arrival of the
Meshiach.) Nevertheless, I left the conference
with a feeling of hope and verve.

There was one question, however, raised by
a mother that made us pause and reflect as to
the nature of our existence:

If the primary purpose of existence is to
fulfill G-d's commandments; and if a Jew is
unable, from childhood, to carry out any of

these commandments because of severe physical
and mental limitations; what then is the
purpose (or meaning) Of his/her existence?
I would be most appreciative if you would
respond to this question.

All our children are entitled to be
educated Jewishly. With G-d's help all our
goals and dreams for our children will become
a reality in our generation.

Once again, thank you for your concern and
understanding.

Sincerely yours,

Robert Wilkes, DSW
Member of Federation's
Planning Committee For
The Retarded - 743-4100 .Ext.
610, 61

P.S. Copies of your first letter written
to me on 22 Av, 5739 as well as your
message and greetings to the conference
participants were included in a kit
distributed to each participant. Enclosed
is a conference kit. Your message was
read by myself immediately after our
dinner on Wednesday, December 10th. We
also learned that you had just a few days
previously endorsed the UJA-Federation
campaign. Both your endorsement and
message generated a sense of excitement
and challenge that enhanced our

deliberations.

cc: Rabbi Dr.Benjamin Sharfman, Chairman Rabbi
Isaac Trainin, Director, Religious Affairs
Committee

RABBI MENACHEM M. SCHNEERSON
Lubavitch
770 Eastern Parkway
Brooklyn. N. Y. 11213

493-9250

מנחם מענדל שניאורסאהן
ליובאוויטש

770 איסטערן פּאַרקוויי
ברוקלין, נ. י.

By the Grace of G-d
25th of Teves, 5741
Brooklyn, N. Y.

Dr. Robert Wilkes
Brooklyn, N. Y.

Greeting and Blessing:

Thank you very much for your letter and for
the Conference kit received separately.
I appreciate the trouble you have taken
to report to me on the Conference and its
recommendations. May Gd grant that the
Conference will produce the desired fruits,
even in excess of expectations. Especially
as the Zechus Horabim helps, particularly
when the Rabim are, in this case, our Jewish
youngsters.

With reference to the question at the
conclusion of your letter, raised by a mother,
to the effect that if the primary purpose of
existence is to fulfill Gd's commandments; and
if a Jew is unable from childhood to carry out
any of these commandments because of physical
or mental limitations; what then is the
purpose or meaning of his/her existence?

The answer to this question must be sought
in the context of a more embracing general
problem, of which the above is but one of many
possible facets.

It should be remembered that according to
the Torah itself, it is impossible for
every Jew, as an individual, to fulfill all

the 613 Mitzvos. Apart from mitzvos which
are applicable only in Eretz Yisroel and
during the time that the Beis Hamikdash is
in existence, there are mitzvos which are
obligatory only to Kohanim for example, while
there are mitzvos which a Kohen is precluded
from fulfilling. But by virtue of the fact
that all Jewish people are one entity, like
one organism, every individual who fulfills
his or her obligations to the extent of their
Gd-given capacities, share in the totality of
the effort and accomplishment.

A similar principle prevails also in every
human society in general, where everyone has
to contribute to the common wealth, though
each one is necessarily limited in one's
capacities, be one a plain farmer, producing
food or a scientist or inventor of farm
machinery and the like. One who excels in
one's particular field of endeavor may be
limited or useless in another area. Who is to
say which one is more important, which one
makes a greater contribution? Only harmonious
collaboration and utilization of all human
resources make for the utmost completeness
and perfection of the society. As for the
individual, all that need be said—as indeed
our Rabbis have emphasized, is that Gd does
not demand of an individual anything that is
beyond the individual's natural capacities.
It is not for a human being to question why
Gd has endowed one individual with greater
capacities than another individual.

To return to the subject of the
correspondence, namely, the needs of the
special children (or the so-called retarded or
developmentally limited, as often spoken of),
they are, to be sure, limited in certain areas
(and who is not?), but there is no reason nor

justification, to generalize all into one and the same category of "limited" or "retarded." Human experience is replete with examples of individuals who have been severely limited in some aspects, yet they subsequently excelled and made great extraordinary contributions to society in other aspects.

I am quite convinced that if a proper system of aptitude tests were instituted, to determine the particular skills of our special children at an early age and appropriate classes were established to enable them to develop these skills, the results would be enormously gratifying, if not astounding. Needless to say, such an educational method would greatly enhance their self confidence and general development, not to mention also the fact that it would enable them to make an important contribution to society.

With esteem and blessing,

M. Schwertan

O.T.S.A.R.
JEWISH ADVOCACY GROUP FOR RETARDED CHILDREN
144-11 70 Road
Flushing, New York 11367
(212) 263-3471

February 26, 1982

Rabbi Groner
Lubavitch
770 Eastern Parkway
Brooklyn, NY 11213

Dear Rabbi Groner,

On behalf of the parents of OTSAR
("Jewish Advocacy for the Retarded")
and myself we would like to extend .a
personal invitation to the Lubavitcher
Rebbe, Shlita to attend our <u>first</u>
Milava Malke, 12 Adar, 5742. Our guest
speaker will be Rabbi Dr. Immanuel
Jakoboviz, Chief Rabbi of the United
Kingdom.

Our friend and colleague, Dr.
Robert Wilkes, has informed us that
only recently one of our parents,
Mrs. P. Gaffney together with Dr. G.
Schwartz and Dr.Wilkes spoke at a Beth
Rivka Parents Association meeting in
Crown Heights on December 8, 1981; and
that the Lubavitch school principals
from Brooklyn have been working
closely with Rabbi Martin Schloss
regarding workshops on 'learning
disabilities' and 'resource rooms' for
either Jewish or English studies or
both.

It was on 22 Av, 5739 that Rabbi
Menachem Schneerson, Shlita sent Dr.Wilkes
a comprehensive and sympathetic statement
that encouraged all of us to <u>include</u> our
special sons and daughters in all aspects of
Yiddishkeit. That letter was the beginning--
the catalyst--which induced other Rabbis and
communal leaders to take a public stand; and
it was again the Lubavitcher Rebbe, Shlita,
who sent us words of support and blessing
when together with Federation -of Jewish
Philanthropies we conducted a historic major
city-wide conference on the needs of our
Jewish developmentally handicapped. Once
again, we come to the Lubavitcher.Rebbe,
Shlita, and the Lubavitch community to ask for
your prayers, your concern, and your active
participation.

Please feel free to contact Dr. Wilkes,
who will I'm certain, be ready and prepared to
do whatever he can to facilitate your efforts.

We hope and pray, with גיב ליבערשטערס help, that
our work in behalf of our special children
will merit the coming of Moshiach.

Respectfully yours,

Y. Tauber